792.8
Wa

Walker

Eyes on the ballet

EYES ON THE BALLET

Few people can become ballet dancers, but many thousands can share the delight of ballet from the other side of the footlights.

This book discusses choreography, décor, music, costume and the history of ballet. But the author differs from other writers of ballet books in approaching the subject from the standpoint of the audience, and showing the many interests linked with a love of ballet: ballet clubs, for example, films, lectures, and collecting ballet material (programs, clippings, etc.).

Eyes on the Ballet will be welcomed because it is not based on the unattainable. It does not say, as do so many ballet books, "You too can be a ballerina," but it tells every girl or boy how they can get the greatest possible pleasure from ballet through their own alert, receptive appreciation.

New York City Ballet in Serenade

EYES
ON THE BALLET

Kathrine Sorley Walker

WITH A FOREWORD
BY DAME ALICIA MARKOVA

Illustrated with photographs throughout

The John Day Company
NEW YORK

AUTHOR'S NOTE

Eyes on the Ballet was first published by Methuen in London in 1963. The present United States edition has been completely revised and appears with a largely new selection of photographs; and I would like to thank various friends in America, and in particular Miss P. W. Manchester of *Dance News,* whose knowledge of ballet in the United States has been of such great help to me in this revision. For this edition, too, Dame Alicia Markova, who more than anyone embodies the link between ballet in England and in America, has had the very great kindness to contribute the Foreword.

K. S. W.

Library of Congress Catalogue Card Number: 65-20733

MANUFACTURED IN THE UNITED STATES OF AMERICA

Second Impression

Foreword by Dame Alicia Markova

There are two kinds of participants at every dance performance. Those behind and on the stage, and those in front of it. Those in front, of course, are the audience and they are very important to all theatrical arts and, most of all perhaps, to the art of dance, which is so specialized and so intricate that it requires an understanding on the part of the spectator to get the fullest enjoyment out of a performance.

It is easy to enjoy watching ballet but the more understanding that can be brought to it, the more pleasure the spectator will receive, the deeper will be his or her love.

This knowledge cannot be acquired too young, for it will grow and grow through the years and be an endless satisfaction for those who are the faithful ballet audience. I know myself, from my own career as a dancer, how much it meant to me that, in my audience anywhere in the world, there were always some people who really understood ballet in its deepest sense. I cherished their letters, and the flowers I would so often receive from total strangers who had enjoyed my dancing and wanted to thank me in this lovely way.

Kathrine Sorley Walker has written this book for the young balletgoer, the real lover of dance who wants to participate in the art by understanding it in all its many areas. She was just such a young ballet lover herself, long before she began to write about it. She took the trouble to learn everything she could over years and years of watching ballet and talking about it, and reading everything that others before her had written.

And now she has put it all down in this book. There is not a single facet of a dance performance that she does not cover, though she freely admits that ballet is her real interest and love, for, being British, it is only very recently that she has had more opportunity to watch modern dance.

She tells how a choreographer goes about the work of putting his ballet together — how he gets his ideas for a story, if there is one; how he works out the steps with his dancers. She discusses the many kinds of music to which dance works are created, the styles of designing which go with the particular kind of ballet for which it will make the framework.

There is much about the dancers themselves, how they study and strive for years, and the rewards which they find in performance. She suggests some of the books that should be read to give the historical background of this great art we love so much.

Her enthusiasm is on every page because she never forgets that dance is first and above all a most beautiful art meant to be enjoyed. She writes as one ballet lover to another, the only difference being that she is much more experienced than those she addresses and she wants very much that they should share her experiences with her, and thereby increase their own enjoyment.

We who spend our lives on one side of the proscenium arch are never unaware of those on the other side. We know that a lot of the applause is sometimes meaningless because it is not founded in any real understanding but is prompted by some surface trick that catches the eye. But there is another kind of applause — the roar which follows a moment of silence — when we know we have established the truest kind of communication and that the audience has somehow understood.

We can never have enough of that kind of an audience. And it is just such a book as this that can help to create another generation of lovers of dance, who love, but love with discernment and understanding.

ACKNOWLEDGMENTS

For permission to use photographs on the pages shown, thanks are due to Martha Swope (frontispiece, 58, 61, 63, 119); Jack Mitchell (45, 114, 128); Louis Mélançon (143); Dominic (41, 79, 127, 132, 160); Roy Round (171); Mike Davis (27, 134); Houston Rogers (33, 35, 48, 56, 71, 75, 117); Central Press (53); Anthony Crickmay (81, 121, 123, 125); Roger Wood (85); Mogens von Haven (112); Paul Wilson (139); Angus McBean (145); Metro-Goldwyn-Mayer (156); the Rank Organisation (158).

Contents

ILLUSTRATIONS

Eyes on the ballet

Both sides of the footlights

PART ONE
BOTH SIDES OF THE FOOTLIGHTS

The halves of ballet are separated by the footlights and the orchestra. On one side are the people who present it: the dancers, choreographers, directors, who create ballets and put them on the stage; on the other side is the audience. Which is "the other half" depends on which side you spend your life. For you and me it is the stage, and the backstage, world; but for the people who work there we, the audience, are "the other half."

Ballet is a partnership — an equal partnership. For us there would be no ballet without the professional artists who provide it; but for them — well, no one composes a ballet and dances it purely for his own personal pleasure without any thought of an audience to watch it. A ballet is not really born until its first night, when the public comes in and looks.

There are plenty of books that tell the audience what dancers are like, what ballets are about, how they are produced and how a ballerina develops. There are books that show us behind the scenes. But this book is going to talk about the other half — the audience — about us; about what we are, and what we do and should do, and how we behave. For once the spotlight will be swiveled around, off the stage and the leading dancers, the bright costumes and sparkling technique, and on to the rows of seats in the auditorium where those of us who love ballet sit and watch. . . .

Every evening now someone, somewhere, has eyes on the ballet. There are families in their homes looking at TV. There are movie audiences watching a filmed performance. There are people in theatres seeing ballet on stage. And although all those of us who are interested in ballet can be grouped into the word "audience," we go on being individual people in our reactions. Ballet gives us pleasure in a great many different ways.

Sometimes you enjoy a film and send someone else along to see it. You tell them it's funny or interesting or well worth going to. When they see you next they say, "Well, I don't know what you saw in *that*. I thought it was awful." Everybody has different tastes, and everyone who watches ballet probably likes it for a different reason — and because there are so many different kinds of ballets they can all find something to enjoy. In *The Mikado* the wandering minstrel has a song about himself, and he says

> *My catalogue is long*
> *Through every passion ranging,*
> *And to your humour changing*
> *I'll tune my supple song.*

Ballet is like that. Its "supple song" can be tuned to amuse us or touch us, to make us think or to show us patterns of lovely movement. If we simply want to look at something beautiful we can go to *The Sleeping Beauty*, and be spellbound by the lovely dances of the ballerina. If we love watching exciting national dances there are plenty in the ballroom scene of *Swan Lake* or in *Coppélia*. If we would rather be stirred and moved by a dramatic story, there are ballets like Dame Ninette de Valois' *The Rake's Progress* or Balanchine's *Prodigal Son*. Whatever we want, ballet can satisfy us. We can be touched by Giselle when she is betrayed by her lover and dies tragically. We can smile at old Dr. Coppélius as he searches for his lost front door key. This is really one of the fascinating things about ballet — there are so many different kinds of ballets, of dancers, enough to keep us all interested for a lifetime, once we start.

But where *does* it all start? Where did it start with you? Most people begin by being taken along by someone else, a friend, someone in the family perhaps. *They* choose the program, and if they choose well, you are converted, you are fascinated. You want to learn more about it and the more you learn the more interesting it gets. The more you think about it the more worthwhile it seems.

With me, it began when I was quite a child. I was taken along by my mother, who loved it — I remember it was to a theatre in London that was destroyed in an air raid during World War II. The company was called the Vic-Wells Ballet — now it is England's Royal Ballet. We saw the ballroom scene from *Swan Lake,* with Alicia Markova and Anton Dolin; we saw *Job* and *The Rake's Progress.* If you have seen *Swan Lake* in its entirety you will remember the six princesses the prince has to dance with at the ball. One of the princesses that night was a young dancer called Margot Fonteyn. And the Usher who tells the prince that strangers have arrived was also quite unknown — his name was Michael Somes, and he later became well known as a principal dancer.

From that evening I loved ballet. A lot of people feel that way, I think. They are immediately enthusiastic; they want to find out everything they can about it; they want to see as much as they can. With other people, of course, it comes more gradually.

If you look around any ballet audience you find people of all types and all ages. There are the ones whose memories go back to past seasons of Russian Ballet, and there are the ones who are there for the first time. There are people who just go occasionally, for an evening out. But there are a great many for whom ballet is an absorbing hobby, and they are the ones who make up the true "ballet audience." It is for them that ballet lives and grows and thrives. They take an intelligent and critical interest in it.

That may not sound important, but it is. If you have ever done any amateur acting, or been on any kind of stage, there is one thing you will have noticed: the difference between all the rehearsals, even the dress rehearsal, and the night of the performance when you have the audience there for the first time. There is a different atmosphere altogether, something rather electric and very exciting, when you know there are rows of people sitting "in front," when you hear laughter or applause as the performance goes on. It would not be the same at all, even if you were in costume and had your make-up on, if the hall were quite empty. A performance needs an audience. But some audiences are better than others. Perhaps your play ran for two nights. Perhaps the audience on the first night did not seem to react very satisfactorily. They may have been slow to laugh; you may have felt you weren't "getting over" to them very well. The next night, however, everything may have gone better. Perhaps some people had been there the night before and got to know the play and knew when to expect the best bits of the comedy. Their laughter set the others off and you felt so stimulated by their appreciation that you found yourself acting better as a result, and so the whole evening was twice as good as the first.

Well, that's the sort of thing that can happen in the professional theatre too, and very much in ballet. When a large proportion of the audience knows a ballet, and is quick and ready to appreciate it, this can influence the rest of the people watching; and then the warmth of this understanding gets over the footlights to the dancers and they react by dancing and acting twice as well as before. Dancers and audience depend on each other. We need the dancers to give us the performances we enjoy, they need us to appreciate them — and to understand them. The more we understand, in fact, the more we shall appreciate. We may begin by just watching; but if we are really going to be lovers of ballet we have some work to do. We must learn something about it, and we must think about it a good deal. In our own way we are as important as the dancers because we are the other half of the partnership.

The first time people go to the ballet they probably come away with a rather incomplete idea of what has happened. It is a little more difficult to appreciate a ballet to the *full* on the first seeing than it is to enjoy a play. In a play we rely a good deal on being told by the actors what it is about. Our ears help us to understand the action. But in ballet we have to train our eyes to do most of the work.

There is sometimes a great deal going on in a ballet. In the ballroom scene of *Swan Lake*, for instance, near the beginning, there is a point where there is a lot to watch, all of it quite important. The Princess Mother and Prince Siegfried are seated on thrones on a dais. All around the ballroom, sitting and standing, are guests from various countries — from Spain and Hungary and Poland and Italy — and court ladies and attendants. Six princesses have been invited and the Princess Mother hopes Siegfried will choose a bride from among them; but he is in love with the beautiful Swan Princess Odette he has seen by the lake that afternoon.

The six princesses begin to dance. Their dance is the thing that an audience would naturally look at — they are in the center of the stage, they are the people who are moving. But if we are to understand what is going on we must not miss the little mime scene that goes on between Siegfried and his mother. He has been very thoughtful and sad, and she rouses him and suggests that he should dance with the princesses. Dutifully he comes down from the dais, dances with each in turn. Then as they continue dancing he moves around the stage — the guests whisper to each other and look at him as he passes by — and stands for a moment, perhaps, at the window, obviously hoping against hope that he will see Odette. After a second he moves on and reaches his mother's side as the princesses finish their dance; and then there is a general mime scene in which he is asked by his mother which one he considers most beautiful, which one he wishes to marry. He replies that he will not marry any of them. His mother is distressed and vexed with him, and the princesses move off, looking very put out.

Now to notice all this detail from the audience means that you have to watch really carefully. You cannot just let your eyes rest on the most obviously arresting thing. If you did you would see the princesses dancing, but you would miss all the essential mime on the part of the prince and his mother and all the building up of the scene through the byplay of the guests.

There are any number of similar instances in ballet. To get the full meaning of any of them your eyes have to be on the alert. They have to see as much as they possibly can. They have to look at the details as well as the full scene. They have to take in what the *corps de ballet* is doing as well as the part played by the principal dancers. *Everything* is important.

That is one reason why people go over and over again to the same ballet. First of all they get a general impression. Then they go on watching it until they have come to know the details. You need almost *all* your senses to ap-

25

preciate ballet. The movement (the dancing and mime) and the décor (costumes and scenery) appeal to your sight; the music appeals to your hearing, and the drama to your emotions and your mind. All the same, we always come back to the eyes. When a choreographer "writes" a ballet — of course he doesn't write it as one writes a letter — he is planning it primarily for people to watch. There will be music to hear and that is important, for there is always a close connection between the music and the action. But the whole meaning of the ballet will depend on what is seen. And when we in the audience look at it we have to look at it in detail, and then we can start thinking about it and about what it means.

DANCING AND DANCERS

Perhaps the best way to begin to understand ballet is to talk a bit more about the elements — the dancing, mime, music, décor — that go to make up a production.

Most of us learn *dancing* of some kind when we are children. When I think of dancing class, I think of a very large room in a big old house with French windows at each end and steps down to stretches of lawn. The floor was wood — not too polished in case we should slip. There was a grand piano and a tall, thin, dark-haired woman sitting at it. The dancing mistress was short and stout, and she had drop earrings that waggled when she moved. She had curly reddish hair and a very commanding personality. She took us through all the elementary exercises,

Classwork at the Arts Educational School, England

and the thin pianist patiently started and stopped, started and stopped the same phrase of music until we could do the series of steps. There was a *barre* along the walls of the room and long mirrors, and sometimes when I was early for my beginner's class I would watch big girls doing their exercises at the *barre*.

That is the sort of scene behind all ballet, behind every dancer all the time. Dancers always have to go to class. It doesn't matter how famous, how expert, they must still do their exercises and practice their steps every day. This is a part of their life forever. And learning how to dance, studying the classical technique of ballet, is never easy. Often a dancer is tired and sore — but you never hear one complain of it.

I think the attitude of this very young professional student (writing unprompted to a friend) is typical:

Yesterday we went to class as fresh as daisies but came out an hour and three-quarters later like dead drooping ones. I was wringing wet from head to foot. My face was like a furnace and I could practically see flames rising from it. When we reached the dressing room we all flopped to the ground and no one spoke for half an hour; then we had to get ready for another class. We worked so hard I thought I was going to die — and when I got up this morning I could hardly move. But I loved it. It made me feel really satisfied, as though it was worth working for. . . .

It is very interesting to watch a professional ballet class. I think the thing that is most impressive is how hard they all work, and how well they take criticism from their teachers. It is fascinating to see what arms and legs and bodies and heads can do — it makes you realize how undisciplined and uncontrolled your own body is. In the beginning you are amazed and full of admiration at all the physical feats of ballet — the leaps and turns that would be as impossible to you as climbing Mount Everest. But when you have become more used to it and seen a good deal of classwork you begin to set less store on multiple pirouettes and difficult lifts for their own sake. You realize that this is part of the dancer's training, just as a telephone operator learns how to work an enormous and complicated switchboard. It is marvelous and very admirable; but you stop being spellbound by it.

That is an important point to reach. Of course some people never get there. They go on being obsessed by the sight of brilliant *pirouettes* and *fouettés* — and of course it is a lovely thing to see them well done, just as it is lovely to see massed bands marching and countermarching or to watch Olympic Games competitions. Any masterly piece of physical training *is* lovely to watch and gives one a real thrill. But there is a tremendous difference between that kind of thrill and the feeling one gets from watching a superb performance of a great dramatic ballet.

Perhaps the first time I realized this completely was when I saw a performance, again by the Vic-Wells Ballet, made up of Frederick Ashton's *Les Patineurs* and *Giselle*. *Les Patineurs,* a delightful ballet, has also been danced by American Ballet Theatre. It is what is called a "divertissement ballet" — that is, a ballet made up of various dances all connected by a theme and a setting. In *Les Patineurs* the setting is an outdoor skating rink, and the dances are all based on the kind of steps and figures ice skaters perform. Now ice-skating is very much a "showing-off," an exhibition of how brilliantly people can do various leaps and pirouettes, and that is exactly what makes the ballet so much fun to watch — it is full of brilliant dancing. The first time I saw it Harold Turner — then one of England's leading dancers — was dancing the Blue Skater (he is called the Green Skater in America), a part he created, a part that threads through all the rest and is always lively and expert. He danced magnificently and was the embodiment of confident charm and ability. The curtain came down to the picture of him spinning, seemingly endlessly, against the background of the white arches, the Chinese lanterns, the snow falling; and the audience burst into applause. It was an example of perfect "virtuoso" ballet — the kind of ballet that shows off brilliant technique and gives you the sort of thrill that Davis Cup tennis or fine show jumping can provide.

There was an interval, and some of the audience probably thought everything would be a bit dull after that. It seemed odd that the program should start with a sure-fire hit like that — it was bound to trail off. Nothing could seem quite so good. Then we saw *Giselle*.

Margot Fonteyn and Robert Helpmann were dancing. *Giselle* is an old ballet about a peasant girl who is in love with a nobleman in disguise. She finds out that he is betrothed to someone else and goes mad with grief and dies. That is Act One. In Act Two her spirit rises from the grave to join the mysterious Wilis, the ghosts of girls who died before their wedding days. The Queen of the Wilis tries to take revenge on the young nobleman and make him dance with them until he dies; but Giselle manages to save him.

That is the story. The music is old-fashioned, but it was written specially for the ballet and so it fits perfectly all the scenes and dances. The costumes and scenery are fairly traditional — the girls wear dresses based on the "ballerina" length dress called the "romantic tutu," and the men wear tights and tunics. It always has a very charming effect — but when two superb artists dance in it, it is very much more than charming. That evening Fonteyn and Helpmann *were* Giselle and Albrecht. The modest, lovely peasant girl who lived in a cottage with her mother and picked grapes with her friends and led them in dances; the gay young count who had run away from the oppressive life of the court and dressed in simple clothes and fallen in love with an unspoilt peasant girl although he was betrothed to a princess — they were both completely real to us. We cared about them passionately, about their happy playful lovemaking, and the tragedy that fell across their lives when the princess and her father came to the village, recognized the count, and told Giselle the truth. Giselle went mad; and there was not a sound in the audience while, pitifully, she tried to dance as she had with Albrecht and remembered with horror that he had deceived her; while Albrecht watched her, powerless to bring her back to sanity, even by the strength of his grief and remorse. Every expression, every movement, every gesture went straight to our hearts so that we shared with both of them in every moment of the tragedy.

This was a different kind of brilliance. This was something quite apart. The mastery of dance technique in *Les Patineurs,* admirable though it was, had been learned and practiced to perfection. The performances of Fonteyn and Helpmann in *Giselle* were certainly based on that same dance technique — they could not have given them if they had not learned and practiced too. But the ballet called for an additional quality — and one that cannot be learned in class — intensity of feeling and depth of thought. And they had *thought* themselves into their parts, and then *felt* so intensely about them that they had drawn the audience into a fine stage experience. All great dancers do this.

That is the standard to aim at. That is the goal a dancer must reach before he or she is really important. She can be very good, she can be technically brilliant, she can be beautiful or charming; but if she cannot dance and mime a great part with feeling and thought she is still not a real ballerina, no matter how she is graded. It is the standard, too, for us in the audience. Once you have seen a performance like that *Giselle* you do not easily enjoy *all* the others. You begin to think, "This is not so good. *They* did that better." You miss all kinds of wonderful touches that brought the characters to life.

When that happens, you realize two things. First of all, you now have a standard with which to compare other dancers. That is important, or else each one will seem as

Alicia Markova and Anton Dolin in The Nutcracker

good as any other. You must keep that standard in your mind. Don't lose it. It's very important to be able to think "*They* did that better."

But you have to remember, too, that the ballet can be done differently. It is far better to have a completely different interpretation of a part, from a dancer of a different personality and appearance, than to have a pale copy of the very best. And a performance can be interesting and well worthwhile even though it is not, perhaps, up to the very highest standard. We cannot always insist on the highest standard, unfortunately! So when we get something a little less good we have to accept that. We have to remember the one that was better — we must keep the difference clearly in our minds; but we have to say, too, "This one may not be superb but it *is* very good. And there are some things about it that are really quite fascinating. It's very well worth seeing."

There are, of course, various types of dancing. Most dancers study all of them at the beginning — you see that from dancing school performances — not only classical ballet but also Latin-American dancing and all the kinds of dancing you get in a musical show. It is really a good idea, because nowadays ballet has very wide frontiers and a dancer may be expected to know every branch of her art — and that art is not confined to *The Sleeping Beauty;* it includes the style of dancing you get in *West Side Story* and the almost acrobatic movements in many of Roland Petit's ballets.

Even in classical ballet you get divisions. The old, set definitions were four in number. There was the *danse*

Margot Fonteyn as Princess Aurora in The Sleeping Beauty *(Royal Ballet)*

→

noble — that is, the pure classic style of dancing such as you get in the "ballerina" role in *The Sleeping Beauty*. There was the *danse de caractère*, the "character" dance, which was a dance in a ballet but based on some national or traditional dance, or expressing some type of character or some occupation. There was the *danse de demi-caractère*, the "partly character" dance, which was a dance with some characterization or meaning but made up of classical ballet steps — there are hosts of examples of *that*. Think, for instance, of the *pas de deux* for Puss-in-Boots and the White Cat in *The Sleeping Beauty*, which shows the character of two cats with their fondling and quarreling but all as much made up of classical ballet steps as Princess Aurora's part. In fact, a great many dances or even complete roles in ballet come under the heading of *demi-caractère;* but it is a very clumsy expression to use all the time, so that often people talk about "character dancing" when they mean "demi-character dancing." Last, there was the mimed role, such as Carabosse in *The Sleeping Beauty,* or the Princess Mother in *Swan Lake.*

Nowadays of course the old divisions are getting less and less apparent, and many dances and ballets are so very mixed up that it is quite impossible to sort them into definitions at all.

Instead it is interesting to think about the various types of dancers you see in ballet now. There are the classical dancers who are capable of such parts as Princess Aurora — a role made up for the most part of beautiful soft movements, some quite slow, perfectly controlled and timed. They are the dancers who stand a chance of reaching the very top of their profession. There are the virtuoso classical dancers, like the Bluebird and his princess, whose dances need speed and balance and are full of turns and leaps and steps where the feet are beaten against each other — the various kinds of *batterie*. There are the dancers who create characters through classical dancing, like Caroline in *Lilac Garden* or the sailors in *Fancy Free* — their parts range from tragedy to the gayest comedy. Caroline's movements all show her gentle nature and her grief at having to give up the man she loved. The sailors' dances in each case reflect their temperaments — exhibitionist, cajoling or sophisticated. Then there are the dancers whose parts are based on national dance steps. These may be short sequences, like the Tarantella dancers in *Swan Lake,* or character studies like Massine's famous Spanish Miller in *The Three-Cornered Hat.* Finally, there are the mimed roles, small ones like the Prince's Tutor in *Swan Lake* and full-length ones like Dr. Coppélius.

Dancers tend to fall into one or another of these categories because of their natural gifts, their physical build, their temperament. But there are plenty of dancers who are a bit of all of them. Generally speaking the qualities overlap. Some dancers can be considered in at least four of the five categories. Two I can think of who have danced most kinds of roles are Nora Kaye of American Ballet Theatre and Pamela May of the Royal Ballet.

On the other hand, while such dancers can give a good account of themselves in a great many styles, they all are probably pre-eminent in only one or two of the categor-

Maya Plisetskaya in Laurencia *(Bolshoi Ballet)*

ies; and with some dancers a type of dancing springs to mind immediately, as with Alexander Grant of the Royal Ballet, whose "character" and national dancing is outstanding, or Melissa Hayden, who is a striking dancer of dramatic roles.

Dancing demi-character parts, although it looks very like acting in ballet, is not really the same. A demi-character part probably largely consists of steps and gestures and movements that the choreographer has designed to show a character, or a mood. For example, the part of the Barber in Massine's *Mam'zelle Angot* has a sequence where the poor little Barber has to watch his beloved Mam'zelle Angot dance with another man, and he is desperately unhappy and his friends try to comfort him. Now the way this is danced is brilliant — but it is demi-character dancing rather than acting. It is all there, in the gestures and steps and the *arrangement* of the whole thing which, of course, is the responsibility of the choreographer. A first-rate character dancer gets the very most out of it; but even with a much less good dancer it would still have a great deal of effect simply because of the way it is put together.

But acting in ballet is making a character live even if the choreographer has *not* given him any distinctive way of moving or behaving at all: the kind of thing for instance that happens with Prince Siegfried in *Swan Lake*. Prince Siegfried need not come alive at all, really. Sometimes he doesn't. He merely walks about and supports his ballerina and dances his variation in Act III. But if the part is taken by a dancer of individuality like Rudolf

Nureyev, for instance, then Siegfried becomes a person. You can tell what he is thinking at various times, what his reactions are, how deeply he feels for Odette, how delighted he is when he thinks he has found her in Odile, and how remorseful afterwards to think he has betrayed her. None of this *has* to show because of the things he has to do. It is something extra, that is added to the part by the dancer through acting, through what we call mime.

Now one definition of mime is that it is a language and it is used to express meaning. There are gestures and scenes of mime that all dancers learn and that can be learned by the audience — in fact it is a great pity if we *don't* learn them. Some are very simple, like the hand-on-heart gesture which means "I love"; some are more obscure, like the twirling of hands high above the head which means "dancing." These gestures can be done by any dancer, even one who can't act at all. If they are done correctly, they will put over their meaning to an audience who knows what the gesture means. But the term "mime" has a wider significance than this gesture-language. It also means acting without speech. It is not even confined to dancers — sometimes straight actors mime rather better than many dancers do. It is the business of expressing things by gesture, by facial expression, by movement, without using your voice. And mime of this kind depends mostly on the natural intelligence and understanding of a performer — it cannot really be taught unless a dancer is good at it naturally.

It is a fascinating gift. It means that a dancer can create a character without very much help from the

The mime role: Margot Fonteyn and Keith Rosson in Swan
Lake *(Royal Ballet)*

choreographer. There are some minor parts that the choreographer has not really thought could make a mark at all, but when they have been danced by a dancer with a real talent for mime they have emerged as characters never to be forgotten by the audience.

What *is* it that makes the character, in the hands of a great mime? A classic example was Robert Helpmann's Dr. Coppélius. It was a character you immediately believed in. There were a hundred small details that fitted into place — details of appearance, of changes of mood, of action. You felt that this was a real person — this old chap living on his own, working at his hobbies, fussy about his things, liking his drink at the nearby inn. All this, you see, is creative work. The basis was there, in the choreography of the ballet; but the character was built up *on* the basis by a great mime. He created the character out of his observation of people's idiosyncrasies, his appreciation of what his fellow human beings are like.

Dancers have to learn other things besides dancing and mime. There is stage presentation, for instance. This means the way the dancer carries herself on the stage, how she walks or turns her head when she is not dancing, how she takes a curtain call, how she adapts her dancing to the size of the stage so that she can keep on a small stage and yet spread her movements to cover a large one. Dancers have to dance in all kinds of places. I have seen the same dance given on a pocket handkerchief of a stage like the little Mercury Theatre in London where the Ballet Rambert began — if you ever saw the film *The*

Red Shoes you saw that tiny hall — and on the huge stage of an opera house, and looking just right in both places because the dancer has adapted her style to fit. It is rather like making a drawing go on a small sheet of paper or enlarging it for a bigger one — or getting an address neatly on an envelope whatever its size. It takes experience to do it easily. The other day I saw a boy dancing a variation at a school show. He did it very well, but it was a fairly small stage with a curtain at the back, and at one point he got rather tangled up in the curtain when he was doing a series of leaps. Well, an experienced dancer would be able to avoid that, and "place" his dance so that it fitted the stage.

Then, too, dancers have to learn how to wear stage costume. That sounds easy, but it is full of difficulties really. It is fairly simple for girls to feel at home in the kind of costume they wear for *Les Sylphides;* probably most of them have at some time or other got into something very like it. But wearing historical costumes or national costumes is different. You have not only got to wear them — you have got to look convincing in them, as if you really were a peasant in the village in *Coppélia* or a lady-in-waiting to a seventeenth-century queen. A peasant and a duchess must not hold their heads and arms alike. Then there are all the little details like using a fan or handling a garland — think of that tricky Garland Dance the girls do in Act I of *The Sleeping Beauty*. All these things need thought and practice to make them seem perfectly natural and easy.

There is make-up too. To a certain extent all women

now know something about make-up because they use it every day. But that is totally different from stage make-up; and ballet make-up, as you can tell if you see a close-up photograph, for instance, is really an art in itself. Actually at its best it is not in the least distorting. A close-up photograph of a really fine bit of make-up is a fascinating thing, and if you study it carefully you see that however unlike the dancer herself it may appear to be it is closely based on the essentials of her face — it is not really unlike her at all, though it may well be unlike her normal appearance. But ballet make-up is exceedingly difficult to apply and there are plenty of dancers who are not very good at it.

Some girls at the beginning of their careers have not had the slightest idea of how to make the best of their looks. Either they have put on too little make-up and looked colorless under the strong lights of the stage; or they have put on so much they have looked bold and unpleasant. Some of them have learned surprisingly well how to improve.

Whenever I have had the good fortune to watch an expert making up I have found it quite entrancing. To sit at the side of some dressing room and see the stage picture gradually, capably, methodically, built up, is an unforgettable experience. The application of a foundation, the blending of tones, the smoothing in of grease-paint, the eye-and-lip make-up — the face is suddenly arresting and vivid, and the off-stage person who sat down to that dressing table has become the fascinating and familiar stage personality. There is a wealth of thought

Melissa Hayden making up as Titania in Midsummer Night's Dream *(New York City Ballet)*

and care, a cool professionalism and tremendous artistry in a perfect stage make-up.

MUSIC

Dancing, mime, and the related points of how you make up and how you get around on the stage — from them we must go on to music. And as far as that goes, it is a great help in understanding ballet to be able to play the piano a little. Any musical instrument would do, really. Even if you can only play the piano very amateurishly, it makes you more capable of appreciating the score of a ballet if you can get hold of a piano arrangement of it and pick out what you can on the keyboard.

If you cannot play any instrument — or even if you can — it is also a very good idea to put on a record of some ballet you have seen once or twice and see how much you can remember of the action from listening to the music. Then go and see the ballet again and work out which scenes or dances are matched to various passages in the score. If you do this once or twice you will probably find you can link them pretty reliably — a bit of music will suddenly remind you of some moment in the ballet. If it is *Swan Lake,* for instance, at one moment you will suddenly, in your mind's eye, see Siegfried waiting for Odette, with the swans lined up down the sides of the stage, and see her run in and pause in a supported arabesque on point leaning on his outstretched arm — and that kind of thing will begin to happen all the way through. Sometimes it is almost as if you switched on a television set. The other day I heard someone else's radio by chance, and it was playing the music from the *Sleeping Beauty* Vision Scene; and immediately I was mentally in the theatre watching the pyramidal group of green-clad nymphs clustered around the Lilac Fairy, while Aurora and Florimund moved around and through them and came together in front of them in a supported arabesque.

When you have done that kind of thing, try to work out one or two other points. Sometimes music is specially composed for a new ballet. Tchaikovsky did this for *The Sleeping Beauty*, Adolphe Adam for *Giselle*. In our own time there have been scores like Hans Werner Henze's for *Ondine* or Aaron Copland's for *Billy the Kid*. If you think about *The Sleeping Beauty*, you will see that in some of the dances, like the Cats' *pas de deux*, the actions of the dancers and the sounds from the orchestra pit are very cleverly — and obviously — combined. At other times it is more difficult to see the relationship of the two, but all kinds of moments will strike you when you begin to look for them: the type of music that accompanies Carabosse's scene in the Prologue, for instance, and the great difference between that and the gentle music for the Lilac Fairy.

Once you begin to get to know what the music sounds like, and what the action looks like, and to put them together, you can play endless games of this kind. It is important to know which scores were specially composed, because there the composer and the choreographer have worked together to the same story and it is a double

47

Margot Fonteyn and Michael Somes in **Ondine** *(Royal Ballet)*

creation. All choreographers do not behave like Petipa, who gave Tchaikovsky very definite instructions for the type of dance and the length of it — so many bars, giving such-and-such an impression. But at least the choreographer and the composer both have in mind the same point in the action.

But the majority of ballets have been written to music that has already been composed for quite a different purpose, and then one has to remember that the choreographer was limited by the existing music. In some ballets there is a point where one feels the end should come before it does — that sounds two-edged, but I am not thinking of bad ballets when one is glad to see the final curtain! I am thinking of the kind where the action comes to a satisfying finish a minute or two before the actual end of the ballet. But probably the music was written first and the choreographer could not simply slice the last bars off; so he had to invent something to use up the time.

Sometimes a ballet written to existing music, however, fits it so perfectly that it is almost impossible to believe the music came first. César Franck's *Symphonic Variations* have been served like that by Frederick Ashton: he has composed a sequence of dances to this score with an unflagging invention that one feels could in no circumstances have been bettered; the music seems even enriched by it. Similarly, Balanchine succeeded in absolutely interpreting, for instance, Bach's Concerto in D Minor for Two Violins as *Concerto Barocco*. A good example of a dramatic ballet composed to existing music is that of Helpmann's *Hamlet*. The music Tchaikovsky had written had a very particular shape of its own. It existed in its own right as a musical composition inspired by Shakespeare's play. But because Helpmann's ballet takes the form of a dream — the dream that might have passed through Hamlet's mind as he was dying, in which he remembered incidents and people out of his life — he was able to create the action so that it completely complemented the music.

There is a third way in which a ballet gets its music, in addition to the specially composed score and the single existing piece of music. That is for someone to select passages from various works, probably by one composer, to suit the story of a new ballet. Sometimes the choreographer does this himself, but more often it is another composer or the musical director of a ballet company. It is very difficult to do it really well, so that it does not seem patchy nor distort the intentions of the original composer.

An excellent example of this kind of thing is *Pineapple Poll* by John Cranko, whose score Charles Mackerras arranged from the Gilbert and Sullivan operas. The theme of the ballet is from one of Gilbert's *Bab Ballads,* about a dashing captain with whom all the women fall in love. All his sailors' wives, and Poll, who sells ribbons and laces, get onto his ship disguised as sailors, and he has a dreadful time trying to explain the situation to the girl he is going to marry. The music for *Pineapple Poll* has been chosen from quite a few of the operas and very aptly, too. For instance, there's a point where the girls are all moping for love of the captain and that dance is set to a song from the opera *Patience* which goes "Twenty lovesick maidens we, lovesick all against our will. . . ."

Another finely-put-together score is the one for Balanchine's *Night Shadow,* devised by Vittorio Rieti from music by Bellini.

Of course, if you know a lot about music already all this will be very evident to you. But if you like ballet and *don't* know a great deal about music you will find that trying to learn something about ballet music will help you to appreciate music as a whole. Ballet has a very wide range of musical accompaniment nowadays. Most of the foremost composers of our time have written scores for ballet, and there is probably not one famous composer whose music is not represented by some ballet score. So if you once get to know a ballet score by a composer you can then go on to listening to his other work on phonograph records or in the concert hall, and get to know his individual style.

DÉCOR AND COSTUME

The last ingredient of ballet is décor — costumes and scenery; and it is very important indeed. Here again, this is a visual element — something for our eyes to study. And all sorts of things happen in the décor for ballets.

There are various broad categories of costume. There are the ones usually called "romantic tutus" — like those in *Les Sylphides:* shaped bodices with low round necks and tiny sleeves, a wide, calf-length skirt made up of layers of tulle. They came into popularity in the nineteenth century, when most of the ballets were about otherworldly creatures like the Wilis in the second act of *Giselle*. They were just right, because they were gauzy and white and shining, and you could easily imagine them belonging to fairies or spirits. But now they come in all colors and for all purposes: basically, for instance, the dresses in the "Prelude" Scene of *Bourrée Fantasque* are romantic tutus, but modified and decorated.

Then when ballets like *The Sleeping Beauty* with their greater technical demands began to be popular in the late nineteenth century the dress was shortened into the "classic tutu," which was more or less like the ones in *The Sleeping Beauty* today, the ones that most people think of as "ballet dresses." In those days they were a bit longer and bunchier, because it wasn't considered modest to have the brief costumes one sees now. Even now, different countries have different lengths for "classic tutus." With both these tutus, the man's costume was based on tights and tunic — and of course many of the most up-to-date ballet costumes are still modern versions of these costumes, the classic tutu and the tights and tunic. Then there is the "flowing drapery" kind of costume. This was influenced by Ancient Greek costume, and you see it now in a ballet like Martha Graham's *Clytemnestra* — short tunics for the men, straight, simple, draped dresses for the women. Variations of the women's dresses find their way into a great many ballets — for instance the costumes for Ondine and the sea spirits in *Ondine* derive

Mary Hinkson in Circe (Martha Graham Dance Company)

from the same source really. There are many costumes which are simply "body-tights" with some decoration; and there are national and peasant-style costumes, such as the ones in Act III of *Swan Lake* and for the peasants in Act One of *Coppélia*.

Most ballet costumes fall into one of these categories, altered of course to suit the ballet. But sometimes you get something quite different. Ninette de Valois, for instance, when she composed *The Rake's Progress,* got the inspiration for her ballet from a famous series of pictures by Hogarth, who lived in England in the eighteenth century; and the costumes for her characters are entirely based on these pictures with only a few changes.

Now the main points about all ballet costumes are that they should be easy to dance in, and that they should present a good stage picture. Everyone knows nowadays that often the most effective stage costumes are by no means the ones that look best off stage. I remember a production of *The Sleeping Beauty* some years ago in which all the costumes, off stage, looked marvelous — beautiful material, exquisite detail and so on. On stage they were ineffective, and not nearly as impressive as another production where everything was mostly flimsy material and bold effect.

It is a difficult business of course to design a whole long ballet: *Coppélia* for example, with many costumes and two or perhaps three sets; and quite often designers are not *completely* successful. They may do well by the majority of costumes and produce one or two atrocities here and there. They may invent unwieldy collars or headdresses that are very difficult to dance in and spoil what we call "line" — that is, the outline of head, body, arms and legs that a dancer makes when she takes up a position. I can remember a good many odd hats and collars and trimmings which must have been a penance to wear on the first night of a ballet, and which have conveniently got lost before the next performance. Sometimes each individual costume is very attractive but put together they are entirely wrong: one ballet I remember had dancers dressed in deep blue, cabbage green, yellow and gray with dashes of red. On the other hand you can put together on the stage colors that do not look well together anywhere else — you can mix up your pinks and yellows and crimsons and scarlets and get a glorious effect.

The best ballet designs have all something strong and definite about them, whether they are rich and detailed and sumptuous, like the famous Diaghilev Ballet ones by Benois for *Petrushka,* or Bakst for *Schéhérezade,* or whether they are deceptively simple and cool. People outstanding in this last line have been Sophie Fedorovitch, who did the designs for a number of ballets danced by the Royal Ballet and the Ballet Rambert; and Irene Sharaff and Oliver Smith, who have done many designs for American ballet.

Sets and backcloths have their own problems. Simple or abstract designs are perfect for a ballet which is all dancing, because then a backcloth is purely a back*ground* which must in no way interfere with the dancing. In fact, for pure dancing you don't have to have any painted or

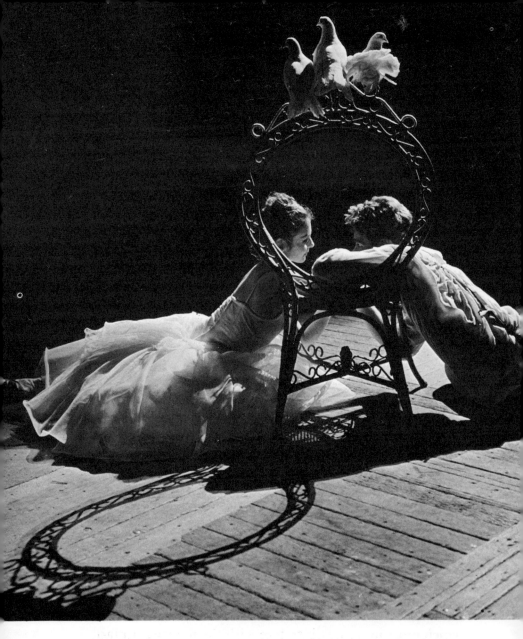

Lynn Seymour and Christopher Gable in Les Deux Pigeons
(Royal Ballet)

designed backcloth to help your impressions — you can have a plain curtain. Sometimes you see a classical *pas de deux* presented with the dancers in simple white costumes against a black curtain — or black against white — and as a result you can appreciate every tiny detail of performance. If the dancers are technically brilliant there will be no flaw in their positions, their timing, their every slightest step or movement; and if, in addition, they are exciting personalities, the technical perfection will have the added sparkle of star quality.

But for ballets that have themes or stories a plain backcloth is not enough. Sometimes you only need something to set the atmosphere. The set for *Lilac Garden,* for instance, is just that — a painted garden full of heavily blossoming lilac trees.

The story ballet, however, often needs more than a *suggestion* of atmosphere. The setting, the backcloth, the drop curtain (which comes down in front) must either fill in gaps or add to the audience's knowledge and understanding in some way. A ballet like *Coppélia* must have its village square, with Swanilda's house, and a house for Dr. Coppélius with a balcony for his doll to sit on, and an inn for Dr. Coppélius to go across to for his drink. The second act must have his workshop with all the other mechanical dolls and various bits of furniture — in fact, you must really have the kind of set you need for a straight play. A drop curtain can be a valuable link and it can also be used for setting the scene of a ballet at the beginning. There is a very fine example of this by Rex Whistler for *The Rake's Progress* — a beautifully drawn

Design for costume in Figure in the Carpet *(New York City Ballet)*

eighteenth-century London street, the kind still to be seen around St. James's Palace, with houses and a church and very real-looking puddles among the cobblestones. A drop curtain, you see, can contribute something that cannot be explained during the ballet — it can tell you the kind of world in which the story of the ballet takes place.

A backcloth for a dramatic ballet can be quite complex without obscuring the action, but the key to that sort of success is often to get the right kind of lighting. Lighting of every kind plays an extremely important part in décor. Shadows can be beautifully used; spotlighting and side-lighting can be very dramatic. There are all kinds of effects that can be got — and one thing to remember is that some theatres are not so well equipped as others with facilities for lighting, so that if you see a ballet in a theatre for which it was not composed it is possible that the lighting may not be as good as it was originally.

To appreciate décor properly, look, if you can, at the artist's designs — sometimes they are shown in exhibitions, sometimes reproduced in books. You will see various differences from the finished product. There will be those impractical collars and hats, the ones that have been discarded. You will see that some designers simply indicate what they want the costume makers to do and leave the drawings in a fairly sketchy state. Others go to enormous pains to put in detail so that their designs are pictures in themselves; and they sometimes even pin little bits of appropriate material to the drawings.

When you have seen a ballet with designs by some

particular artist, have a look, if you can, at his other paintings. Ballet design, like ballet music, can lead you on to other branches of the art; from an artist's ballet designs you begin to take an interest in his pictures, just as from familiarity with a ballet score you may come to appreciate a composer's concert works. And of course anything you can learn about historical costume, or about color and design and the building up of groups, will help you in appreciating the look of a ballet.

CHOREOGRAPHY

And now what about choreography? It is not easy for the onlooker to learn about and yet in some ways it is the most interesting thing in ballet. Most of the time the audience is only aware of a general effect. But if you go a lot to ballet and see one ballet over and over again the detail of the choreography becomes visible.

Choreography is a tricky and complicated thing to explain. The choreographer has really two main jobs: he has to create the action of the ballet and link it up with the music and the décor; and he has to teach the parts to the dancers and produce the ballet generally. He is the key man. There could be no ballet at all without him. There would just be isolated elements — there would be a story or theme, there would be a musical score, there would be costume and scenery designs, there would be dancers. He has to fuse them all together to present on the stage to *us*.

Design carried out: Mary Hinkson and Arthur Mitchell in
Figure in the Carpet *(New York City Ballet)*

A choreographer is usually a dancer himself (I speak of "himself" but there are of course some very fine and famous women choreographers, among them Dame Ninette de Valois and Agnes De Mille). He may not be an outstanding dancer, but he has (I think always) had practical experience as a dancer with a ballet company. Otherwise he could neither plan the steps nor teach them to the dancers. He has to have a good understanding of music, and a good understanding, too, of painting and design — although in both spheres some choreographers are more knowledgeable than others. But apart from that, choreographers are like writers of books — all different.

Some choreographers are mainly interested in the setting of dances, either the sort of *divertissement* you get in the last act of *The Sleeping Beauty* — various kinds of dances for one, two, three or more dancers — or in continuous dancing to a musical score such as you get in Balanchine's *Concerto Barocco*. Other choreographers create dramatic dancing and movement to express a story, making a kind of "play without words," such as you find in Eugene Loring's *Billy the Kid*. Now that is a ballet about the notorious outlaw who lived on the Mexican border, and in a ballet like this the choreographer creates his characters, develops the story and produces the big dramatic moments just as if he were writing a play; but it is all done through the medium of classical ballet technique, and so it is just as much a ballet as *Concerto Barocco* or *The Sleeping Beauty*.

Now the difficulty for us in the audience as far as choreography is concerned is that we have to train ourselves

Choreography: George Balanchine rehearsing Suzanne Farrell and Jacques d'Amboise (New York City Ballet)

to discover exactly what the choreographer has contributed to the ballet. It is not like a play that we can take home and read. But the choreography of a ballet is, as it were, the play that is printed and bound up into a book — the play without the actors' performances. Compare a ballet — say, *Billy the Kid* — with a play by Shakespeare — say, *The Merchant of Venice*. In the play, when it is in book form, you get the scenes, the action, and the characters set down in words — that is, the contribution of the playwright. In the ballet, if it *were* possible to get it in book form, you would have every step, movement and dance that makes up the scenes, the action and the characters — that would be the contribution of the choreographer. In the play, if you saw it staged, you would also get *performances* by actors — they would say the words in certain ways, they would add to the words of the characters their own particular interpretations and their own facial expressions and make-up. In the ballet on stage you would also get *performances* by dancers who would add to the basic movement *their* own interpretations and expressions.

But with the play, even after seeing it in the theatre, you could look it up in the book and study the foundation on which the performances of the actors were built up. You can't do that with a ballet. You can't take the choreography home and see what it is like without the performances — you have to do the next best thing and get to the point where you can separate the elements of a ballet.

Now that sounds very difficult, but it isn't impossible.

If we are really to know a ballet we must be able to see how the various elements — the choreography, the music, the décor, the dancers' performances — work together to get the general effect. Take them apart in your own mind — it sounds cruel, but anything that's really worthwhile is always capable of standing up to being analyzed. Hold them apart just long enough to see for yourself what they each consist of — how one effect comes from the music, one from a particularly striking costume or background or type of lighting, one from a sequence of dance steps or a way the dancers are grouped, and one from an individual performance. Then let them click back to make their proper complete picture once more, and you'll find that picture stronger and more compelling than ever.

That type of treatment is one of the ways the audience can serve ballet. Ballets and dancers are all far better for being discussed and dissected and thought about. And any ballet company is all the more interesting for having a large number of people in the audience who go regularly, because it is the "regulars" who are sufficiently interested to discuss them. Of course there are disadvantages in "regulars" too; but to go a lot to ballet, if you think about it as well, is a good thing both for yourself and for the dancers. It makes you gain an extra sense — delicate, like a seismograph — that notes fluctuations in standard; you get a sort of tolerance that makes you realize that performances must be better sometimes than at other times — there can be no absolute level; and you get to know what constitutes a really superb presentation.

When Shakespeare was writing his plays for the Globe Theatre he had that sort of audience. They came regularly; they got to know the actors and their capabilities. They could appreciate his topical references, and they watched his plays with lively, critical affection. That is the kind of audience you sometimes get for ballet. I was part of one during World War II, when the Sadler's Wells Ballet danced in London at the New Theatre. It was a reasonably small audience, and there was a majority in it of people who had just that sort of love and appreciation for the ballets and the dancers that Shakespeare's audience had for his plays. Because the company knew quite well how keen and knowledgeable our interest was, because we were quick to react, they were spurred on to do their very best, so that we got interesting new ballets and exciting performances. A similar audience exists for New York City Ballet on its home ground, and an audience like that always stimulates an artist to good creative work. It is a beautifully tuned instrument on which he can play, and it is the kind of audience that ballet thrives on, the kind of audience we can do it most good by becoming.

There are two different ways to approach ballet. We should approach it through our minds — give it thought, learn about it, apply our intelligences to it. But we should never forget to approach it with our hearts too. As ballet is indeed a partnership, in which dancers and audience are dependent on each other, it means that just as the dancers give out to us performances full of feeling, of sparkling comedy or moving tragedy, so we must be ready to appreciate them, and laugh or weep with them. In theatregoing we must give in order to get.

PART TWO

Ballet and its development

PART TWO
BALLET AND ITS DEVELOPMENT

If we go to ballets often and look at them carefully and talk about them to other people who are interested, and think about them ourselves *and* give them our enthusiasm and love, we are well on the way to being a good audience! But any real hobby and interest must be studied. If you're enthusiastic about watching any sport you are eager to know as much as you can about it — not only the names and styles of players of the moment but the important players in the past and how the game has developed and what it is like in other countries. If you are a stamp collector you buy catalogues and find out about stamps all over the world and their histories and values. It would be a dull sort of hobby if you didn't. And going to ballet involves you in a hobby about which there is a tremendous amount to find out.

The past is always important though you can live your daily life without thinking very much about it. But probably at one time or another you have almost automatically taken an interest in the way things used to be. Old-fashioned railway engines, automobiles, the little airplanes of the 1920's, the silent movies, styles of clothes — all these things, in every sphere of life, are part of our background. We should not fly by jet, we should not have the latest screen epic, if there had been no early versions. And we should not be ourselves if it were not for our grandparents and our great-grandparents, and so on right far back. Every single thing in the present has developed out of something or someone in the past. It is exactly like that with ballet — only even more obviously than in many other cases.

Plenty of books give the history of ballet in detail. I am not going to attempt that here — but there are one or two simple little lines of development you can get clear in your mind.

Think back as far as you can into that haze of yesterday — back to primitive man and to the tribal dances — they are still to be seen in parts of the world, Australia, Africa, the Americas. . . . Dancing begins with primitive man but ballet of course does not. Dancing goes on, through the religions of the Far East that were cultures long before Greek and Roman times, it goes on *through* Greek and Roman times, it continues right on to the sixteenth century — dancing by people either for their own pleasure or as part of their religion or as a kind of society grace. Then it took on another form: it began to be presented by people as an entertainment for other people, and that was the beginning of ballet.

Look back to the year 1581. In England Elizabeth I is Queen. Shakespeare is still an unknown young man,

Nadia Nerina and David Blair in La Fille Mal Gardée: *an eighteenth-century ballet revived with new choreography (Royal Ballet)*

walking across green Warwickshire fields to see Anne Hathaway. In France the court is celebrating the marriage of a princess of Lorraine, and a clever Italian has arranged an entertainment of dancing that he has called "a dramatic ballet in honor of the Queen" — the word ballet, you see, comes from the Italian *ballo,* a dance, *balletto,* a little dance.

That ballet had all our ingredients — but they were so different that *we* have never seen anything like it. The dancers were not professional ballet dancers, trained in classical technique — they were courtiers. The dancing was fairly slow and stately because it was based on the social dancing of the time. The music was played on instruments that were the ancestors of ours. The setting was the hall of a great palace, not a theatre stage, and the audience sat on three sides of the space cleared for dancing. The costumes were what we think of as "Elizabethan" — farthingales for the women, doublets and hose and short cloaks for the men, ruffs for both — from our point of view very much a stage costume. But the people in the audience then were dressed just like the dancers. To them it must have felt as it would to us if our dancers wore modern evening dress. The only difference was that the dancers wore headdresses or masks to show the characters they were representing.

Ballet looked like this for a long time; but eventually the fairly simple steps of the dances were added to by more complicated ones, and because courtiers could no longer cope with them professional dancers began to be employed. Some of them were recruited from companies

of actors, or touring bands of acrobats; and naturally
when the ballets were performed by professional dancers
they could be made more interesting. All kinds of new
steps were invented. And the new ballets demanded a
theatre, with a proper stage and some measure of lighting
and scenery.

Gradually the classical technique of ballet was built up.
To begin with, only men took part in it, just as only men
and boys acted Shakespeare's plays. It was not considered
the thing in the sixteenth century for women to appear
on the stage. But fairly soon the women got in, and it was
the influence of women that changed the costumes from
ordinary dress to something different. Marie-Anne Cupis
de Camargo, one of the greatest early ballet dancers,
shortened the skirts of her dresses so that she could move
with more speed. The heeled court shoe gave place to the
soft flat dancing slipper, for the same reason.

But not only costumes were being improved. Various
dancers and choreographers were developing the ballets
themselves. One famous ballet master, Jean-Georges
Noverre, worked at theatres all over Europe in the eighteenth century, and he is a good example of how a lively
mind can influence an art tremendously. He had all kinds
of sensible ideas — some of them so completely adopted
now that it seems strange to us that he had to suggest
them. For instance, in those days there was a custom that
instead of a dancer putting over a character by his mime
and facial expression and movement, he wore a mask
showing what the character was meant to be. Noverre

laughed that practice out of court. All the same, some of his criticisms could still be made today. He deplored, in his *Letters on Dancing and Ballets* which were published in 1760 (you can get a translation and read them for yourselves), that there were so many ballets where "dancing is introduced for the mere sake of dancing," because that kind of entertainment was not really a ballet at all: and there are of course still a number of ballets that are perilously near the description of "dancing for the mere sake of dancing."

Noverre pointed out that a ballet should "speak to the soul through the eyes" — that ballet had a higher purpose than simply to show off difficult and exciting steps to make an audience applaud, or offer them some clever acrobatic dancing to amuse them. Ballet is an art, and an art must be capable (to quote Noverre again) of "inspiring, moving and captivating the spectator": in other words, it should make us think as well as feel.

After Noverre, in the early part of the nineteenth century, ballets began to be based on very romantic stories — stories like that of *Giselle* or *Ondine* about princes and sea spirits or supernatural beings like the Wilis; and the ballerinas began to wear the "romantic tutu" we talked of earlier, and to dance on the tips of their toes, *en pointe*. To begin with, the shoes were only slightly reinforced with stitching, and Marie Taglioni, the first Sylphide, for instance, only stayed on her toes for very brief spells — just long enough to give an effect of fairylike lightness. But gradually the toes of the shoes began to be "blocked"

The Sleeping Beauty *(Royal Ballet), first produced by Petipa in St. Petersburg in 1890*

— that is, strengthened properly, and of course from that moment ballet began to be very much more like ballet as we see it now.

To know what ballet was like in the Romantic Era you have to think of *Giselle*, which was first produced in 1841 in Paris. Its story is typical. Its music is typical, too — pretty, dramatic, always full of delightful little melodies that are easy to listen to, reflecting exactly what is going on. The style of the choreography, too, is a good example of its time. There are scenes of mime which tell the story, set between solo dances or *pas de deux* for the principals, and dances for the *corps de ballet*. These were meant to serve as a rest for the ballerina and the *premier danseur*, but they also help to create the appropriate atmosphere. In the first act the gay peasant dances give the village life, and in the second act the gliding veiled shapes of the Wilis set a mysterious background for the moment when Giselle's spirit is conjured up from the grave.

The next step, after the Romantic Era, was to the kind of ballet you see in *The Sleeping Beauty*. It was the direct result in some ways of those properly blocked shoes, because dancers were able to do astonishing feats of technique, and in order to show these off the costumes were shortened to the "classical tutu" — and as a natural result the romantic creatures like the Wilis gradually vanished.

Because of the fascination of the new techniques *The Sleeping Beauty* has far more dancing than story — which was not the case in *Giselle*. The music is of a higher order. Adam's music is just right for ballet purposes; but Tchaikovsky's scores are worth hearing even when we have no dancers to watch, and are sometimes played by orchestras as part of a concert program. Indeed, plenty of people who have never seen the ballet of *Swan Lake* love its music. *The Sleeping Beauty* was produced in 1890 at the Maryinsky Theatre in St. Petersburg (now the Kirov in Leningrad) with choreography by Marius Petipa, and it was typical of its time — very spectacular and very brilliant.

Ballet continued to develop. The next development was toward a different kind of ballet, the short ballet such as *Les Sylphides* (1909) or *Petrushka* (1911). These ballets were the work of a choreographer called Michel Fokine. He felt that once more ballet was getting to the point that Noverre had deplored over a hundred years before — it was becoming "dancing for the mere sake of dancing." That is a danger that always threatens the ballet, a battle that has to be fought over and over again. All the exciting new steps that had been invented were making everyone forget that ballet should "speak to the soul." People were more interested in applauding technical feats, like the thirty-two *fouettés* in Act III of *Swan Lake*, than in appreciating ballet as a whole. One ingredient, dancing, was queening it over all the others. Fokine wanted to bring things back so that dancing, mime, music, décor and choreography were once again equal partners.

He worked for a famous company, the Russian Ballet directed by Serge de Diaghilev. Diaghilev, who was not a choreographer or dancer himself, had a particular genius. He was able to bring together choreographers, composers, designers and dancers so that remarkable ballets could be put on stage. Everything that was most interesting in the artistic life of his time came together under his direction into the service of the ballet. In the ballets Fokine composed for the Diaghilev Ballet he followed out his principles, and we can see the results today. Nearly all the short ballets of our time come in a direct line from either *Les Sylphides* or *Petrushka*.

If you have seen both *Les Sylphides* and *The Sleeping Beauty* you will realize the difference between them. *The Sleeping Beauty* is long, full of dances of all different kinds, and leaving a thousand different impressions. *Les Sylphides* is short, it is completely harmonious, it has what one calls an "entity" — that is, a single personality. You can say about *The Sleeping Beauty*, "I liked the last act best" or "I liked the forest scene most." But with *Les Sylphides* you either like it as a whole or you don't. Although it is made up of waltzes and nocturnes and preludes they all fit together so perfectly that when we think of it we have just one impression — of drifting dancers in shining white dresses, like spirits in a moonlit glade. It began a new style of ballet — if it were not for *Les Sylphides* we would certainly not have our modern *Symphonic Variations, Concerto Barocco* nor even *Les Patineurs*.

Just as *Les Sylphides* is the forerunner of such modern ballets as these, so *Petrushka* is the forerunner of all our modern short dramatic ballets. *Petrushka* was a remarkable innovation. Instead of the story being made the excuse for a great deal of dancing, this time the dance and mime and dance movement were used in order to tell the

Petrushka *(Royal Ballet), first produced by Fokine for the
Diaghilev Ballet in 1911*

story — the story was the important thing. The story is a touching, fantastic tale of three puppets, the Ballerina, the Moor and Petrushka, who is a kind of Russian pierrot. The Moor and Petrushka are rivals, and Petrushka always gets the worst of it both from the Moor and from the tyrannical Showman who owns the puppets. That would not matter so much if it were not that Petrushka is a little more than a puppet — he feels and suffers and loves and eventually is killed by the Moor.

Petrushka was so successful that it is a landmark in ballet history. Not only was the story the important thing, and every action on the stage was planned to *tell* the story; but instead of simply having a *corps de ballet* which merely filled in the time between the principals' dances or made a kind of background (like the garland dance or the nymphs in the forest in *The Sleeping Beauty*) Fokine made each member of his crowd in *Petrushka* a living character. The scene is a market place with a fair going on; and the coachmen and the nurses, the peasants in from the country, the ladies and gentlemen strolling around, the gypsies and the old man with the long beard are all characters and all have their particular part to play in the picture as a whole.

Instead of having what one might call "danceable" music, like Tchaikovsky's for *The Sleeping Beauty*, this score (which was specially composed by Stravinsky) is dramatic music that creates the atmosphere and is an accompaniment to the story as well as to the dancing. The costumes and scenery too are in keeping — there are no "tutus" for the women, no tights and tunics for the men. The people

Merle Park and David Blair in Mam'zelle Angot *by Leonide Massine (Royal Ballet)*

are dressed as if they really had walked onto the stage from the streets of St. Petersburg. In every way it is a convincing work, and it is a dramatic story told through dance and mime; and from *Petrushka* have developed our present-day dramatic ballets, such as de Valois' *The Rake's Progress,* or Agnes De Mille's *Fall River Legend.*

Nowadays we take it as one of our standards for a first-rate ballet that the action, the music and the décor should suit each other perfectly — what we call "making a homogeneous whole" — and it is largely due to Fokine that we do.

Another development, from Fokine's ballets, was the renewed importance of men in ballet. Men's parts had tended to get less and less important from the moment women began dancing; and at some stages, in fact, women were dancing men's parts, looking like principal boys in English pantomimes — and of course when they did you could hardly have all the feats of partnering we are accustomed to. But Fokine had in particular two magnificent male dancers, of very contrasted capabilities, and he used them to the full. One was Vaslav Nijinsky, who sometimes seems an almost legendary figure. He was the first Petrushka, and he first danced *Le Spectre de la Rose,* the ballet about a girl who dreams that she dances with the spirit of a rose she has worn at a ball.

The other dancer was Adolph Bolm, who was a particularly fine character dancer and created parts like the Warrior Chief in the *Dances from Prince Igor* or — a strong contrast — Pierrot in *Carnaval.* Since then men have always been important, and not only as what might be

called "ballerina's props." They are equal in importance
to the ballerinas, which is exactly as it should be. It would
be a very bad thing for ballet if they were once again to
become *less* important.

They not only returned to all the "hero" parts (like
Franz in *Coppélia*) but made their mark in other ways.
Very shortly, in fact, after these Fokine ballets, Leonide
Massine came to the fore as dancer and choreographer,
also with the Diaghilev Ballet. And he introduced a variety of roles for male dancers. He put on stage characters
like the Peruvian in *Gaité Parisienne* and the Hussar in
Le Beau Danube, widely expanding the possibilities in
ballet. Massine was a pioneer, too, in creating ballets to
symphonies — remarkably successfully in such cases as
Choreartium to Brahms' Fourth Symphony or Berlioz'
Symphonie Fantastique; but one factor above all in his
choreography was a fresh breath of life — lighthearted
comedy. It is the Massine of *La Boutique Fantasque* or
Le Beau Danube who is unique in ballet history.

So ballet has traveled from the Court in France, by way
of the Romantic Ballet, by way of the Maryinsky Theatre
and *The Sleeping Beauty*, and by way of the Diaghilev
Ballet, to the present day. And while the Diaghilev Ballet
was launching all kinds of new ideas and new artists, classical ballet was being carried to the ends of the earth by
that marvelous dancer, Anna Pavlova, and her company.
She toured extensively and wherever she went an audience for ballet, and potential dancers and choreographers,
were created.

Most present-day ballet companies probably have some

of these "key" ballets I have mentioned in the repertoire: not a court ballet, of course — but they will have *Giselle* and *The Sleeping Beauty* (either as a whole or in part — the part called *Aurora's Wedding*) and *Les Sylphides* and perhaps one of Massine's ballets. So you can have a look at them and see the process of development right in front of you.

Modern ballets really fall into three groups. There is the divertissement ballet. That probably starts off or ends up your program — *Les Patineurs* or any other ballet that is made up of separate but connected dances. A divertissement is a term for any set of *disconnected* dances, like a dancing school show, for instance — dances not linked in any sort of way, a Spanish dance next to a tango or a classical variation. A divertissement *ballet* is made up of *connected* dances, dances all deriving from one theme like skating, or lovers' meetings, but with no sort of story — just a series of dances for various numbers of dancers.

Then there is the plotless ballet, like Ashton's *Scènes de Ballet* or Balanchine's *Symphony in C.* It is not a divertissement ballet. It is composed of continuous dancing, none of which can be taken out of its context and done on its own, all closely linked together and flowing into each other. There are a great many ballets in this category. Finally, there is the dramatic ballet already mentioned: but even that separates itself into two — the ballet with a very slight story indeed and the ballet with a complete and detailed one.

Ballets without plots depend entirely on the excellence of their dancing. They have no mime because they have

Divertissement ballet: Anya Linden and Desmond Doyle in
Les Patineurs *by Frederick Ashton (Royal Ballet)*

no story to tell. The dramatic ballet on the other hand sometimes has almost as much mime as dancing, because the characters have to be created and the story made clear to the audience.

All these types of ballet are equally good and important. Before you have got very far in talking and reading about ballet you will come across various statements saying that one kind of ballet is better than another, that some types are not ballets at all. The reason for this is very simple and human. Everyone likes one kind of ballet more than another, in the same way that people like different books to read, or spending their vacation in different ways; and quite a number of them get into the bad habit of saying that the kind of ballet they like themselves is very much better than any other kind. That of course is nonsense. It is part of the charm of ballet that all these kinds exist side by side, and we can see all three sometimes in one evening. It is a lot more interesting to try to enjoy them all, and appreciate their differences, than simply to like one and dislike the others.

READING ABOUT BALLET

The hobby of being interested in ballet does not stop at going to performances and watching ballets. There are other things you can do about it. You can read about ballet — books and magazines and newspaper reviews. You can see films about ballet. You can collect and look at photographs. You can make up what one might call your own archives. You can listen to talks, you can take part in discussion groups, you can go to exhibitions. In fact everyone who gets really interested in ballet has, in the words of the old song, "a job for life"!

I can remember when there were relatively few books about ballet. With a little perseverance one could have them all, or at least read them all. It is a bit more difficult now because there are so many. It is hard to know what to choose. . . .

In a way, the best books to start on are probably the books about people actively connected with ballet, or the books written by dancers. One of the very first ballet books I read — and I can remember sitting in a garden by the Rhine in Germany while I read it — was a book about Nijinsky written by his wife Romola. It was a fascinating story, about the boy who leapt into world fame when he leapt off stage at the end of *Le Spectre de la Rose.* Nijinsky had a marvelous ability for covering the ground and for seeming to pause in the air. Romola says: "He crossed the whole stage from front to back in a single bound." Cyril Beaumont describes it as "a rose colored flash — no flurry, no strain — just as though a rose petal had been caught up by a night breeze." Tamara Karsavina, the ballerina who was often Nijinsky's partner, quotes Nijinsky himself as saying, when asked if it was difficult, "No, no! Not difficult. You have just to go up and then pause a little up there."

Nijinsky could dance other parts too. He was the creator of Petrushka and no one has surpassed his excellence in it. Petrushka is admittedly one of those demi-character parts that are so worked out by the choreographer that if a dancer does the actions he must make much the right impression. But all the same no one has ever danced Petrushka as Nijinsky did — never caught the curious spirit of the inarticulate creature, the puppet who can feel but who has no intellect and very little reason. Photographs of him show all the pathos and helplessness in the sad little Slav face and the limp body and limbs. Then you turn over the pages and see other Nijinskys — elegant in *Le Pavillon d'Armide*, passionate as the Negro slave in *Schéhérazade* — and you get an idea of his range and capability.

The story Romola tells in this book is a fascinating and a tragic one. Perhaps she is sometimes unfair to other people in it. If you are passionately concerned with someone it is very difficult *not* to be a little unfair to other people. It is up to her readers to think of all this while they read, and her book is valuable for the vivid world she portrays in it.

A different sort of book, but an even more essential one if you are to understand the *people* concerned in ballet, is Karsavina's *Theatre Street*. It is the story of a life of extreme importance to ballet written by the dancer herself — and marvelously written. Here is part of her description of the very first time she went on a stage, as a very small girl at the Maryinsky Theatre in a pupil show:

I had a feeling that all were looking at me and admiring my costume. I stepped lightly, with a springy step I did not know myself to possess. On the stage all was bewildering;

the audience looked like a black gap beyond the haze of footlights. The lights and the space made me somewhat giddy . . . it did not matter to me how insignificant my part as long as I was in this fascinating stage-world. . . .

Karsavina describes her childhood in Imperial Russia, her days of dedicated schooling at the Maryinsky Theatre; she tells of the great ones of ballet at that time, she describes her life with the Diaghilev Ballet — and incidentally gives a different view of Nijinsky and Diaghilev. From her you can go on to Arnold Haskell's book *about* Diaghilev and find all three — Karsavina, Nijinsky and Diaghilev — once more, seen from the outside. And you can wind up by reading the exciting and enthusiastic account of one man's discovery of ballet in Cyril W. Beaumont's *The Diaghilev Ballet in London.*

You can never go by one person's opinion in ballet. Each worthwhile personality has many different faces. Different people get different impressions. One account is never enough. You have to take two or three and try to work out for yourself what the real person was like.

Of course ballet as it was in Imperial Russia or in the Diaghilev Ballet is not the same as ballet nowadays. The picture of ballet today is much more diverse — it is not just one or two but a number of companies of very different styles. In the U.S.A., two distinctive ballet companies come to mind: New York City Ballet and American Ballet Theatre. From the personalities involved in these companies have come some fascinating books. Agnes De

Mille, for instance, with *And Promenade Home* and *Dance to the Piper*, has epitomized the American dance impulses of her generation. One company has dominated the history of ballet in England — the one whose fascinating story started at the Old Vic Theatre in 1931 when Ninette de Valois presented a program of ballets. Her little company grew into the Vic-Wells Ballet. Then it was called the Sadler's Wells Ballet and is now known as the Royal Ballet. This is a more imposing title than it sounds. It means that the company was granted a charter by Queen Elizabeth II which allowed it to be known as "The Royal Ballet."

Of all the personalities and dancers who have made up this remarkable company, it is Ninette de Valois herself who is the most important. She has written two books, both well worth reading. One is called *Come Dance With Me*. In it, as Karsavina did in *Theatre Street*, she tells us about her childhood — this time in Ireland (her real name was Edris Stannus) — and about her early career. Then she gives a very clear impression of what was happening to ballet in England in the period between the two wars, and writes about the people she worked with in building up the Royal Ballet. The four outstanding names in this connection are those of Margot Fonteyn, Frederick Ashton, Robert Helpmann and Constant Lambert, the composer and conductor; and in *Come Dance With Me* de Valois gives sketches of their personalities as she has found them.

For a short time de Valois was a member of the Diaghilev Ballet. In her earlier book, *Invitation to the Ballet*, she has written a good account of the experience, from the moment she was told to learn *Les Sylphides* and dance "one of the two 'miseries' — an appropriate company nickname for the two *coryphées* who lead the *corps de ballet* throughout." Pages like that make it possible for the audience to understand the point of view of the dancer better, almost, than anything else. A great many dancers are not very articulate — they pursue their art, but they do not write or talk about it in a way that helps non-dancers to understand. So when you *can* read books of this kind — or listen to talks by dancers and choreographers — you bridge the gap a bit; for there *is*, to some extent, a gap.

The dancer sees ballet very differently from the member of the audience. That is bound to be the case. It is interesting to discover how ballet looks to the people who make and dance ballets. All the same, it is not *our* view and we must not forget it.

So we have to go on from books by and about people in ballet — there are of course many more of them — to books about what ballet is and how ballet seems to the audience. The easiest ones in this group are the picture books, and there are various sorts of pictures. There are portrait studies, often taken in photographers' studios, of dancers in certain parts; there are action photographs taken during a performance; and there are posed photographs taken in the theatre. As records of a ballet, from the technical point of view, these last are often the best.

All the same, action photographs have a great deal of value — they actually catch definite moments during performance, and some have in fact been very fine photographs as well. Recent books in this connection are *The Dancer's World* by Michael Peto and Alexander Bland, and Jack Mitchell's *American Dance Portfolio,* both splendid collections. On the whole, action photographs are very satisfying. They really take you back to the theatre, fling the curtain up before your eyes, and start the music in your ears. You see in them what you *saw* — and that is a priceless thing to happen in an ephemeral art like ballet. But to a certain extent that can be said too of many "still" photographs taken at photo calls. On the whole they do not so often get collected into *particular* books, but many of them appear as illustrations to books on ballet. Portrait studies are invaluable, among other things, in recording make-up.

As you study books or magazines you will get to know plenty of photographers' names and can work out for yourself the ones that seem to you most consistently satisfactory.

De Valois' *Invitation to the Ballet* is a book which is only partly reminiscence. It is really more a book about the art and the economics of ballet (that is, the practical business side of running a company); and it is one of the books that stimulate thought and argument. There are others that do it too. Sometimes a book will surprise you into a discovery yourself. I remember when I was first interested in ballet reading a book by Rayner Heppenstall called *Apology for Dancing.* The thing that came out and hit me, as it were, was the way he talked so enthusiastically about "beautiful muscles." I had a rather unrealistic attitude to dancing in those days, and it had never occurred to me to get excited about muscles; but as the years went on I began to be more and more of his mind. It is not of course that the muscles should *show*, but muscular control and discipline are absolutely vital in first-rate performance.

Another sphere where books are invaluable is in learning about the past. One of the books that make the past come most alive is Cyril Beaumont's fine selection and translation of writings by Théophile Gautier called *The Romantic Ballet*. In it we get very human snippets of reaction to the famous dancers, to Marie Taglioni (the creator of *La Sylphide*), Carlotta Grisi (the creator of *Giselle*) — or Fanny Elssler. We get an account of how Gautier thought up the scenario for *Giselle* after reading a book about Germany, and how he planned a ballet called *La Péri*. It makes very good reading, and to go with it there is a magnificent book of lithographs collected by Cyril Beaumont and Sacheverell Sitwell, called *The Romantic Ballet in Lithographs*. The two together bring a whole era before you.

One of the finest sources of information about the ballet in the past is Mr. Beaumont's *Complete Book of Ballets* and its succeeding volumes. He would be the first to agree that they are not *absolutely* complete! But then nothing could be — there are far too many ballets; and these books, with their particulars about ballets and dates, their accounts of action and general comments and biographies of choreographers, are quite invaluable.

In two books, *The Ballet Called Swan Lake* and *The*

Ballet Called Giselle, Mr. Beaumont has also collected together remarkable pictures of single ballets — their origins, their action, their history. These are not exactly readable books; but they are well worth dipping into and referring to. An invaluable pocket guide to productions is Walter Terry's *Ballet.*

Once you start looking for books on a certain subject or a certain period you will find what you want fairly easily, and discover the types of author. Arnold Haskell has given us the word and the book *Balletomania,* and in the book *Dancing Round the World* there is a delightful picture of Russian ballet just after Diaghilev, when the company run by Colonel de Basil had three wonderful "baby" ballerinas (girls in their early teens): Irina Baronova, Tamara Toumanova, and Tatiana Riabouchinska, as well as the adorable Alexandra Danilova. I never saw that company, but I did see all these dancers when they were just a trifle older. My first excursions to ballet were to see them. Toumanova was my first Giselle, Baronova my first Odette, Danilova my first sparkling Swanilda, Riabouchinska my first shining and delicate Prelude in *Les Sylphides.* Haskell brings back these performances to me when he writes, but I think he would *create* them for you, in the sort of way Beaumont creates the Diaghilev Ballet for *me,* and they are certainly worth knowing about.

Cyril Beaumont we have talked about, as historian, critic and devotee of the Diaghilev Ballet. Ivor Guest's books on the past make good reading, especially perhaps, *Victorian Ballet Girl* (about poor Clara Webster whose clothes caught fire on stage and who died from the effect of the burns) and *The Dancer's Heritage*. There are excellent books about the Royal Ballet and the Ballet Rambert (*Dancers of Mercury*) by Mary Clarke and by P. W. Manchester (*Vic Wells: A Ballet Progress*, which is a very personal but very lively account of the development of the company). Walter Terry's *The Dance in America*, Anatole Chujoy's *The New York City Ballet*, Bernard Taper's biography of George Balanchine, the books already mentioned by Agnes De Mille, and John Martin's *World Book of Modern Ballet* report on the U.S. scene; while books like Nureyev's autobiography and Albert Kahn's *Days with Ulanova* provide fascinating insight into ballet in the U.S.S.R. If you want a book about mime there is an excellent one by Joan Lawson. If you want one on costume design there is Beaumont's delightful *Ballet Design Past and Present,* or *Dressing for the Ballet* by Joan Lawson and Peter Revitt. On technique there is *A Manual of Classical Dancing* by Beaumont and Stanislas Idzikowsky, and Kay Ambrose's lighthearted *Balletomane's Pocketbook.* On choreography there is Arthur Franks' considered review of contemporary choreographers in *Twentieth Century Ballet.* Regina Woody has written a delightful series on all kinds of dance in America, while Italia Mara's *So You Want to Be a Dancer* and Agnes De Mille's *To a Young Dancer* will tell you exactly what learning to be a dancer means.

All these writers and the other critics who have published books know what they are talking about as far as facts go; they have all watched ballet enough, and long enough, to be listened to, they are all "authorities." But

95

they are all human beings and they all have their personal likes and dislikes, so when it comes to their opinions on particular dancers or ballets of course you have to make up your mind. You have every right to your *own* opinion. What you can gain from them all is a knowledge of the facts, a professional attitude of mind towards ballet, a reminder of the variety of ideas and reactions people can have, and the stimulus of arguing and agreeing or disagreeing with worthwhile minds.

On the whole, magazine and newspaper writing on ballet is rather *less* worthwhile, but there are one or two magazines that are bound to prove useful to you. There is the English periodical that ever since 1910 has stood as a record of the dance scene throughout the world: *The Dancing Times*. It has held throughout its life a unique place in dance writing. In the U.S.A. *Dance News* or *Dance Magazine* takes the place of *The Dancing Times*, although neither was founded so early, and there have been the splendid series of *Dance Index* and *Dance Perspectives* that deal with one particular facet of ballet at a time. Two other magazines are produced in England, *Dance and Dancers* and *Ballet Today*. They print good pictures and have a wide coverage of news and views. News reading is important because all balletgoers tend to become parochial, to care only about their own particular neck of the woods. Views in magazines, as in books, must be taken with care — and never absorbed without thinking!

Newspapers and general periodicals have ballet critics, of various capabilities. They divide themselves up into the ones who are primarily music critics, the ones who are ballet critics proper, and the reporters who are not special-ists but are just covering the event. It takes only a short time to discover which is which, and you can safely disre-gard the notices written to catch the interest of the public which only rarely goes to ballet. (Remember, though, that it is not usually the critic, but an assistant editor, who puts on the headlines: you may get a sensational headline on a serious notice.) As far as the others — all the others — are concerned, do not accept them as gospel. Think for yourself — and remember, everyone, and that includes every ballet critic, makes mistakes of judgment sometimes.

If you want to read about ballet — books, magazines or newspapers — you do not *have* to rely on buying them yourself or on gifts from your friends and family. There are reading rooms, and fairly comprehensive sections of ballet books, in most of the public libraries; and if the books are not on the shelves you can fill out a card and the library will notify you when the book is in. The New York Public Library on Fifth Avenue at 42nd Street has one of the finest dance collections in the world. It is in a special department with all kinds of rare treasures, pic-tures and memorabilia as well as books, now housed in the Library and Museum of the Performing Arts at Lincoln Center. There is a list of some useful books at the end of this book; and new books are always reviewed in the ballet magazines.

Unfortunately ballet books are usually pretty expensive to buy. But you can sometimes get copies at reduced rates, if you keep an eye open when you pass bookshops. Quite a number of mine have been acquired that way. . . .

AUDIENCES FOR BALLET

All this reading about ballet does not of course take the place of seeing it. This, as a bald statement, sounds like nonsense. But just as there are some people who imagine it is enough to read Shakespeare's plays at home rather than to see them in the theatre, where he meant them to be, so there are people who think you can learn about ballet from books with only an occasional visit to a ballet company. They are wrong. If you are going to learn about ballet you will do it in the theatre, sitting in the audience, waiting for the thrill when the curtain goes up, watching what goes on, watching, watching . . . and thinking. Everyone who ever learned anything about ballet learned it this way. They went to performance after performance. They were not content with seeing a ballet once, or a dancer's performance once, or one dancer in a particular role. They went over and over again; they went until they knew exactly what was coming next all the time . . . oh, but I can hear you stop me and say "But then they wouldn't enjoy it!"

The answer is that if you are seriously interested in the theatre, in ballet, you would enjoy it all the more. A really good ballet wears very well. You can know it thoroughly, you can have seen it very many times, and still be moved by it — not every time, perhaps: that will depend on the performance; but every time it is performed as it should be.

In fact every ballet whose worth is living and permanent (and without fairly frequent seeing, of course, that is a point one cannot decide) has something of the quality of a fairy tale that a child hears with joy over and over again. The first bars of the music are the "once upon a time" that opens a magic gate, and to hear them is to give oneself over to familiar beauties. Indeed it is one of the tests of a good ballet — a work that does not merely impress at the first seeing but is still full of satisfaction for heart and mind at the fiftieth.

It is never ridiculous to go a lot to ballet. Plenty of people who feel it is, find pleasure in some other constantly repeated act. They walk a certain way to see some home or tree or garden that pleases them, they reread a favorite book, they eat a favorite meal. It is really no different to go and see a favorite ballet. You do not get tired of it basically. But of course (given an unwise number of performances crammed into a short period or a dropped standard in performance) you can get stale.

There was a season when the Royal Ballet gave solid blocks of *The Sleeping Beauty* in London, admittedly with different casts, but the same ballet night after night, week after week. It is all very well to say we should have stopped going to see it, but that is not the way the real balletgoer reacts! It was an incredible relief to turn to a mixed program of modern ballets. Ballets like *Les Sylphides* or *Swan Lake Act II* are usually very badly served, because they are nearly always in the program on occasions when everyone goes — first nights of new ballets or of seasons, or special performances; and one frequently gets stale over them.

This is a point managements never seem to understand

or to do much about, and they never seem to realize that even to give various dancers a chance they should never have ballets performed inadequately if they can possibly help it. Quite often they let some dancer try a part; he or she proves quite unsuited to it, but continues to do it and destroys the general standard of performance in that particular ballet. I expect you have seen some ballet that you enjoyed very much for a while, and then later on found it not nearly so effective. It may well be that some particular part has let the whole thing down. There is a ballet I have mentioned already, Antony Tudor's *Lilac Garden*, which has a very delicate magic. It is about a girl in the early years of the century who is being parted from the man she loves and forced into a "marriage of convenience." The man she is marrying is also having to give up the woman *he* loves. They all meet — and finally separate — in a garden full of lilac trees in bloom. Now this is a very intense and beautiful ballet and when it is really well done it is exquisite. But I have seen it sometimes when one dancer — and perhaps only one — is miscast, and cannot put over his or her part with the right deeply felt, poetic quality. Then the ballet, from being a masterpiece, seems to be ineffective. Now on both occasions the ballet itself is the same. The choreography is the same, the music, the décor and most of the performances; but one dancer wrong, and the whole effect is lost; and someone who has never seen it before will be unimpressed, and someone else who was once impressed will say "it hasn't worn well."

There are many factors contributing to anyone's attitude to a ballet. If you do not enjoy something, do not immediately blame the ballet itself; consider whether it is the fault of one of the dancers, or whether the music is not being as well played, or whether you yourself are not in the mood for it, or whether the general audience is not as receptive as it sometimes is.

This last is a point that often has a good deal to do with the impact made by a ballet: the receptiveness of the audience. Just as no two performances of a ballet are alike, so no two audiences are alike. But they fall, I think, into four main divisions.

There is the matinee audience, composed largely of women and children: variously aged mothers and their variously aged sons and daughters (mainly daughters). The mothers often wear little theatre hats and veils (pernicious things to sit behind, as you cannot see the dancing properly) and the children often rustle about in boxes of candy (pernicious things to sit in front of, as you cannot hear the music properly). The merits of the matinee audience depend a good deal on what ballet is being given. If it is *Coppélia* it can be fun to have a preponderance of young children, who are audibly thrilled over everything and shout shrilly and applaud heartily every time they have an opportunity. If it is any more serious ballet their lack of attention and understanding can make it a dreadful experience for the rest of the audience and (I feel sure) for the dancers. Audience reaction is very keenly felt on a stage. There is nothing more stimulating than a responsive audience, whether for comedy or tragedy. And so a matinee *Coppélia* can reach heights because of the stimulus of children's delight, but a matinee *Lilac Garden*, to the accompaniment of candy and inattention, can be a disheartening ordeal.

The next audience I tend to think of as a "learner" audience. By "learner" I really mean an audience that has no chance of seeing a great deal of ballet — the kind of audience you get, perhaps, in a town where companies only appear occasionally — an audience that probably has no previous knowledge of the particular ballets or dancers but is keen to know more. It is a good audience. They take it seriously, they think about what they see, they make up their minds. They are intelligent, but like most learners they are feeling their way to their reactions. Often they are wary to the point of appearing unenthusiastic; and as I said earlier, when an audience is quick to appreciate, their warmth acts as a spur to the dancers; a bit of enthusiasm on the audience's part is essential for a really sparkling occasion. So the "learner" audience never pushes a dancer to a superb performance, and never sees a ballet at its absolute best.

Then there is the gala performance audience, which has a great deal in common with the matinee audience. It is made up in the main of people who are there because it is a social occasion with high-priced tickets to help some charity. Everyone gets into evening dress (of varying grades of stylishness). Sometimes the honors for glamor go to the men — at least if, as at the Royal Opera House, Covent Garden, they wear uniforms and decorations and court dress. I treasure the memory of a diplomat with a beautifully trimmed and pointed beard, a cloak with an upstanding collar, and the star of some order hanging round his neck on a scarlet ribbon. . . . But as an audience, the gala performance one is useless. Very often it hardly bothers to applaud. It only wants to look at itself and be looked at. To waste any ballet on it apart from a divertissement of show pieces, like the brilliant *pas de deux* from *Don Quixote,* is ridiculous, because it leaves its mind at home with its everyday clothes.

The audience which has a preponderance of "regulars" — I spoke of it before when I was talking about Shakespeare's audience — is my fourth category, and I must admit to a special love for it, exasperating as it can be sometimes. It is the one that you and I belong to, even though we do not agree with everyone else in it or even with each other; because it is the audience that watches ballet a lot and knows the dancers' names and capabilities (not just the star dancers either) and is really at home. It is made up a little differently for each company, but it is largely interchangeable. Probably we each have a company we are especially fond of, but we go and see them all and take an interest in them all as well. Without doubt, during our lives we will each have a little group of dancers we are especially fond of — but that certainly shouldn't lead us to shut out all the rest.

For myself, for instance, my company is the Royal Ballet. This is no reflection on the merits of all the other companies I have seen, nor on the infinite pleasure many of them have given me. I have thoroughly enjoyed other British companies, or American companies or French,

Danish or Russian. But watching them I am not, as it were, in my own family; rather, I am spending a holiday with them *au pair*.

Your company will be conditioned by how old you are, and where you live. Enthusiasm in ballet is a little bit like a relay race. Each generation has its loves. In the 1940's my contemporaries and I were hotly defending our dancers against the loyal memories of an older generation; now we, in our turn, are older than you, and our dancers are not yours; and you will find, in time, that you will stand where we do. . . .

The "regular" audience can of course be rather a trial to both dancers and managements, because of its possessive attitude towards a company. When it has watched a dancer over years, possibly from a first appearance, it feels it knows her (or him); and in fact it does know a great deal about her strength and weakness, her ability for dealing with the unexpected, and her general character. In some cases it is only a step from that feeling to the taking of all kinds of liberties that are only possible between friends.

The regular audience often hopes to dictate to the management in the matter of repertoire, casting, prices and so on: it rarely wins, but it never fails to hope it may, and it is strongly of the opinion that it ought at least to register its opinion. And that, to my mind, is not a bad thing. I am well aware that managements are not always wrong; that they frequently have really excellent reasons and motives for doing what they do; but neither are they always *right*, and in a great many cases a little less conviction on their part that the regular audience is mad and not to be attended to might lead to a healthier state for ballet. . . .

Some people are mercifully able to concentrate on a performance without in the least worrying about the audience around them. They can shut their ears to the rustling of paper, the sucking of candy, the opening and closing of handbags, the whispered comments and questions among their neighbors, the various noises that intrude from outside. You are very lucky if you can, because all these things have a very bad effect on your enjoyment. All the same, of course, the more sensitive you are yourself to disturbance the less likely you are to cause it without thinking — which of course is why other people make a noise. They don't do it deliberately; they just don't consider the effect of it on their neighbors and even the dancers. Many people nowadays, through watching television and going to films, are out of the habit of thinking about the effect on a living stage performance of countless small disturbances. There is a nice story, no doubt apocryphal (and nothing directly to do with ballet) about — I think it was — John Barrymore. He was playing Hamlet at a matinee somewhere and two women in the front row of the stalls were having a nice cozy time with tea on a tray. The noise of teaspoons disturbed his soliloquy, "To be or not to be . . ." So he broke it off, and, being athletic, jumped down from the stage and advanced on them, rubbing his hands and saying delightedly, "Ah, tea! That's good!" Sounds *do* reach the stage, even if actors and dancers normally ignore them. . . .

There is one more problem in audience reaction: applause. Now customs vary in different countries. In Denmark in the 1930's, to quote de Valois, "a large and extremely attentive audience was witnessing a performance primarily conspicuous for the most exhilarating display of vitality possible to imagine on the part of the company but at the end . . . the audience rose and left the theatre; there was no applause and no raising of the curtain." In England and the U.S.A., however, audiences have always applauded, and it would sap a company's vitality if they didn't. Perhaps we shout out less than Continental European audiences, apart from some bravos and an occasional booing; but we do clap. I think, in fact, that we clap far too much. Ideally, *Les Sylphides* should go through with no intermediate applause, and the second act of *Giselle* should be uninterrupted by salvos of clapping. The dances are not so many variations, but a sequence of dancing intended to build up a mood; and audiences should be content to let the mood build up, and not make themselves felt by applause.

Nor should they be so impressionable that they can't let *any* technical fireworks pass without applause. The other evening, for instance, I was at *The Sleeping Beauty* and the Bluebird variation was excellently danced; but the audience began applauding at the first spectacular leap and kept it up off and on throughout. That doesn't make sense. All it means is that some people want to show, very loudly, that they can appreciate the difficulty of such a step: but how many equally difficult but less showy steps and *enchaînements* do they *not* recognize? They are really showing off, not their superior knowledge, but its limitations.

But it catches on: the semi-educated who start it affect the completely ignorant, who can see the step looks exciting and that to clap is apparently the thing to do; and so all the rest of the performance is punctuated by tedious applause. The net result of this sort of thing is, of course, that the exhibitionist dance gets a colossal reception and the more restrained, but equally difficult, one is coolly received. A running commentary of applause is the kind of thing acrobats expect and get, but it is totally out of place in the ballet theatre.

Then there is the horrid habit (and this is a vice of the regular audience) of trying to get some dancer an extra call because a previous soloist has had one. Admittedly it is a temptation, if a dancer you do not care for or do not think particularly good gets called back twice, to try to push your favorite dancer's total up to at least three. But it is a baby's game, really, and gets no one anywhere. It can even be embarrassing for your favorite. . . .

In the end, however, everyone just has to bear applause. An audience as a whole cannot be controlled, and there will always be enough semi-educated, or violently partisan, people to bring about these situations. What one has to aim at is that at least each one of us as individuals should think hard about this point, and decide what his responsibilities are. Why is he applauding? Because it is a custom? Because other people started it? Because he knows that particular step is difficult — but does he know all steps, and can he possibly be consistent and applaud every difficult step well done? Because he likes one dancer and wants to fling down the glove to the supporters of another? Or because he is moved, and inspired, and wants to show his gratitude? If the last is any part of the reason, the applause comes at the end of the ballet, where it should.

Of course we are all human; and of course no one is entirely innocent in this sort of test, if he is really honest. But whatever you do about applause, do it with thought; and do it with consideration for the dancers. On the whole, if they are experienced, they have a pretty shrewd idea of what applause is worth. They know that what brings the house down on one occasion falls completely flat on another. They know that we in the audience are sufficiently ignorant to applaud them as wildly when they are bad as when they are good; and they take their standards (at least if they are wise) from their teachers and colleagues rather than from us. But it adds to their problems when they have to contend with either foolish or partisan applause.

Different kinds of ballet

PART THREE

DIFFERENT KINDS OF BALLET

Within the wide framework of classical ballet there are considerable differences in detail. It varies, for instance, under the influence of national temperament. That becomes obvious if you see visiting ballet companies, and compare them with your own.

There are classical ballet companies in countries as different as England, Russia, Denmark, France, and the United States. And although they all dance ballets based on the same classical tradition, they each have a distinct character of their own.

Let us try to work out the differences. Denmark, for instance, is a small country with a tradition of peaceful development; we think of it as being friendly and charming, gay, not very sophisticated — a country of fairy tale castles, and of Hans Andersen and *his* fairy tales. Now a good deal of this is borne out when you go to performances by the Royal Danish Ballet. They have in their repertoire long traditional ballets which they have danced for a century, ballets often based on fairy tales. One of

Napoli *(Royal Danish Ballet): Anette Amand and Niels Kehlet*

these is *Napoli,* which is about an Italian fisherman and his bride who are separated by a water sprite with the comical name of Golfo. This was first put on by them in 1842 and the choreography is by a ballet master called Bournonville whose work was known very little outside Denmark until the Royal Danish Ballet began touring. It is full of gaiety and charm — and it has some fascinating stage tricks. There is a scene when Gennaro rows his boat onto the stage just as if he were really rowing into a little bay; and there is a moment when Teresina's costume is somehow changed in a split second right in front of our eyes in the middle of the stage. It is done so quickly that we cannot discover how: it looks like magic — and it *is,* of course — *stage* magic!

One of the most perfect examples in the Danish repertoire from the point of view of their own typical contribution to ballet is a ballet called simply *A Folk Tale.* It is long, and quite enchanting. In it you really begin to see the national flavor the Danes have brought to classical ballet. The story is about two girls changed in infancy — the heroine has been taken from the manor house to live with the trolls in the mountain, and the trolls have put one of their own kind to live in the manor and grow up as heiress to the estate. Of course it ends happily with things the right way around. Any choreographer might select such a subject and make a ballet out of it but only the Danes would do it in quite the way they have. They have allowed a whole evening to it, but instead of padding it out they really do let a great deal happen. There are plenty of interesting characters too. There are of

American Ballet Theatre in Lilac Garden

course the hero and heroine and the beautiful bad-tempered changeling; but there are two brother trolls who are acted in an extremely individual way, and their mother, and a neighboring landowner who is a bit of a villain, and an old nurse, all of whom really make a mark. There are not only the largely danced scenes when the spirits of the mist appear on the mountain, or the divertissements at the wedding, but a mimed scene when the heroine dreams about what happened to her as an infant, and a wonderful scene when the trolls feast in the mountain. The theme is certainly very Scandinavian and in style the ballet is not a bit like *Giselle* or *Swan Lake* — and, because Denmark is a democratic country, the hero is only a landowner and not a count or a prince.

The .Danes, then, present classical ballet with light-heartedness and simplicity. They give it a sort of wholesome charm; they are particularly interested in good characterization and have some superb mimes; their ballets and performances are refreshing and well-balanced, and very pleasant entertainment.

None of this can really be said about French ballet. Certainly, France is a complex country and people disagree a good deal as to what her national characteristics are; but in her classical ballet at least one might settle for imagination, for passion, for wit, for a love of technical acrobatics and for a piquant contrast of sophistication and simplicity.

Although the major French company is at the Paris Opéra, the best examples for all these qualities come from the companies Roland Petit has directed; because at the

Opéra the company is so international in its influences — it has had foreign *maîtres de ballet* and choreographers and leading dancers so often — that it is of Petit's companies that you think where French national qualities are concerned.

To begin with, take *Les Forains*. This was the first Petit ballet to make a great international impression in 1946, and a more delightful one it would be hard to find. A band of strolling players comes wearily on stage, puts on its show — a kind of circus with clowns and ringmaster — to a small audience which, at the end of it, slinks away as the hat is taken around and leaves the players to pack up and go on again, wearily. That is just an outline — the ballet itself was composed with great imagination and subtlety. It balanced nicely the way the players behaved as themselves and the way they "did their turns." And probably no choreographer or company other than a French one would have managed that ballet to quite such good effect.

Then you get something completely different, like *Le Jeune Homme et la Mort*. This is about a young man who hangs himself in a Paris attic, and everything is rather grim and sordid and very compelling. The unpleasantness is quite unrelieved — and probably only a French choreographer would have been quite so hardbitten over it.

A third type of French ballet, the light comedy ballet, is almost more suited to be in a revue than on the ballet stage. On a first seeing it may be very funny, but it palls later — and a true ballet comedy will make balletgoers

Roland Petit in his ballet **Cyrano de Bergerac** *(Ballets de Paris)*

laugh for years! A revue number is only out to impress fleetingly and once, whereas a ballet should be a lasting pleasure for some reason or other, something you want to see more than once or twice, whether it is for its drama, or its beauty of dancing, or its sheer fun.

Most of the particular qualities of French ballet are found in a ballet Petit composed on the theme of the famous French play *Cyrano de Bergerac*. There is a scene in a kitchen, where chefs and cooks have a series of brilliant dances. It has plenty of sophisticated wit and of acrobatic technique. There is a scene in a garden where the large-nosed Cyrano woos Roxane on behalf of his better-looking friend, and *that* has a good deal of balletic passion. There is a scene where the men go off to war: a little group of women and children and old people stand to one side and the soldiers arm themselves, and take up their banners, and move off in procession, pausing here and there to say farewell to their loved ones — and *that* has great imaginative simplicity. All in all, *Cyrano de Bergerac* is one of the ballets that probably only the French would do quite in that way, mixing up the scenes of the kitchen and the garden and the march to war; and it has nothing at all of the straightforward charm of the Danish productions.

The French and the Danes, however, have one thing in common — they both foster the art of *pantomime,* of mime as distinct from dancing. The Danes have a "pantomime" company which performs, in their open air theatre in the Tivoli Gardens in Copenhagen, traditional mimes, mostly based on the Commedia dell'Arte charac-

Plotless Ballet: Suzanne Farrell and Melissa Hayden in Concerto Barocco *(New York City Ballet)*

ters of Harlequin, Columbine and Pierrot. The French have one or two notable mimes and mime companies — perhaps the most internationally famous name at present is Marcel Marceau.

In ballet the U.S.A. has three first-rate and very varied companies: New York City Ballet, American Ballet Theatre, and Jerome Robbins' Ballets: U.S.A., though this last does not function on a permanent basis.

New York City Ballet, now housed in the New York State Theatre at Lincoln Center, grew up from the American Ballet and Ballet Caravan through the combined vision of Lincoln Kirstein and George Balanchine. In most people's minds it is, in fact, identified with the personality of George Balanchine, who is not an American but a Russian — he was with the Diaghilev Ballet. During over thirty years in the U.S.A., he has created a vast number of ballets in various styles, ranging from the dramatic *Prodigal Son* to a plotless masterpiece like *Symphony in C,* but one of his most distinctive beliefs is that there is enough drama in a ballet if you get two or more dancers onto a stage and show their contrasted styles and temperaments and abilities. You don't need a theme or story as well. There is of course truth in this. It represents the excitement one feels from any great *pas de deux* brilliantly danced. There is truth in most of the wildly conflicting beliefs people hold about ballet, and you have to decide for yourself which belief you feel drawn to by watching the works that express it, and deciding whether you like them or not. Beliefs, over everything in life, are extremely individual. Everybody has his

Kay Mazzo and John Jones in Afternoon of a Faun *(Jerome Robbins' Ballets: U.S.A.)*

own. The attitude of trying to get other people to think
as you do is the one that made the Spanish Inquisition
and every sort of civil war that ever existed. We each have
every right to think as we do.

So some people feel that the plotless ballet in the hands
of Balanchine is the very best type of classical ballet there
is, and some people prefer, say, the styles of Agnes De
Mille or Jerome Robbins. The work of these choreographers is perhaps more typically American. Agnes De
Mille, for instance, has put on productions like *Rodeo,*
which is a picture of a ranch with all the characters belonging to it — the roughriders and buck jumpers and
cow-girls — and the choreography gives a remarkably
good impression of rough riding, in fact! *Rodeo,* too, put
square dancing on the stage. She also composed the less
successful *The Harvest According,* inspired by a line of
Walt Whitman's, "Life is the tillage and death is the
harvest according," about birth and courtship and death
against an American Civil War background.

Another native American theme was used by Eugene
Loring in *Billy the Kid;* and Agnes De Mille, again, took
a violent American story for a ballet — Lizzie Borden's
trial for the murder of her parents in a place called Fall
River — and titled it *Fall River Legend.* (The real Lizzie
Borden was, of course, acquitted.)

Jerome Robbins' ballets have an inventive modern
quality that is immensely stimulating — there is the
sparkling early comedy that pictures American sailors on
leave, *Fancy Free,* the tranquil lyricism of *Afternoon of*

New York Export, Op. Jazz *(Ballets: U.S.A.)*

a Faun; the hypnotic movement of *New York Export, Op. Jazz.*

What are these American choreographers adding to classical ballet? Different sorts of rhythm, for one thing; suggestions of jazz or of square dancing; a blending of high spirits and comedy; different types of characters — all distinctly American in idiom.

As for Russia, it is in some ways more difficult to see her particularly national characteristics, because we have had so much Russian influence on our ballet that the styles are very much entangled. All the same there are many differences. There are even differences in the way the dancers dance — if you see the films of the Bolshoi Ballet and the Royal Ballet you get a good general impression of this. Even when they are doing the same steps (in *Swan Lake,* for instance) their arms and backs and heads and legs behave quite differently.

Apart from this, there is the really national feeling of some ballets — the particular Russian quality, which mixes vigor and languor, West and East, the civilized and the barbaric. *Petrushka* linked Russian street life of the early nineteenth century with the grotesqueries and pathos of the puppets. *Firebird* combined the fierce and the poetic legends of Russia. However sound, technically speaking, a non-Russian performance of them is, their real magic is never present. And no non-Russian company can dance the magnificent *Dances from Prince Igor (Prince Igor* is an opera), with the mingled warrior dances of the Polovtsians and the graceful circling of the Persian women, without losing all the sweep and power

Alla Sizova and Yuri Soloviev in The Stone Flower *(Lenin-grad State Kirov Ballet)*

and vitality of it and making it, somehow, a little embarrassing and a little comic. . . .

The English have their own national character, and at times it has been very apparent in their ballet. They are guardians of tradition and lovers of history. They preserve their old buildings and keep up ceremonies like Trooping the Colour (the military parade on the Queen's birthday), or the State Opening of Parliament; and in ballet they have shown this quality in the way they have preserved and fostered the long traditional ballets. *The Sleeping Beauty,* for instance, had slipped out of the international repertoire. It was only danced in entirety in the U.S.S.R. and in the 1920's and 1930's what happened in the U.S.S.R. was relatively unknown to anyone outside it.

Back in 1921 the Diaghilev Ballet put on their famous and fascinating production of *The Sleeping Beauty* at the Alhambra Theatre in London but in spite of everything it was a financial failure. No ballet company attempted to give it again in entirety until February 1939, when the Vic-Wells Ballet made a notable effort and revived it. To bring a ballet like that back into the repertoire needs people who are dedicated to ballet history. It needed someone like Constant Lambert, the musical director of the Vic-Wells, to get the score in order; it needed the combined memories of various choreographers and *maîtres de ballet* and dancers to revive the dances; it needed a lot of research from everyone concerned. Of course even then it did not please everyone! There were — and always will be — disputes about the order of the dances

Margot Fonteyn and Rudolf Nureyev in La Bayadère *(Royal Ballet)*

Dramatic ballet: American Ballet Theatre in Billy the Kid

and their choreography and the names of the fairies, and endless other points; but basically the ballet was the ballet Petipa put on at the Maryinsky Theatre in St. Petersburg in 1890. So the world owes this revival of *The Sleeping Beauty* — and it has met with very wide success in America as well as in Europe — to the English genius for preserving and respecting — and even re-creating — traditional things.

Perhaps the other main national characteristic of the English is their aptitude for the short dramatic ballet and for what can be called the "literary ballet." That means a ballet based on a work of literature — on a novel, or a play, or a poem. De Valois has done ballets on the *Book of Job,* on *Don Quixote;* Helpmann on *Hamlet* and *Elektra;* Ashton on *A Midsummer Night's Dream* and *Romeo and Juliet;* Andrée Howard on David Garnett's *Lady into Fox* and Keats' *La Belle Dame sans Merci;* John Cranko on *Antigone;* and Kenneth MacMillan combined two novels in his *The Invitation.* Other nations have, of course, contributed occasional dramatic and literary ballets — but in England quite a large proportion of the repertoires of the Royal Ballet and Ballet Rambert have been in this category. (Incidentally, if you ever see a "literary ballet," read the book and see how well staged you think it is.)

By a "dramatic ballet" I mean a ballet like de Valois' *The Rake's Progress,* about a young man in the eighteenth century who comes into a fortune, squanders it and ends up in a madhouse. It is a grim story; but the ballet has a good deal of humor in the early scenes, and the whole production is magnificent choreography. I mean, too, a ballet like Helpmann's *Miracle in the Gorbals,* which has its scene in the slums of Glasgow, and is about a Stranger who brings back to life a young girl who has drowned herself, but is killed himself in the end. But of course a dramatic ballet does not have to be a tragedy — it can be like John Cranko's *Pineapple Poll* which is fun from beginning to end.

The companies that make up the present English scene are, first, the Royal Ballet: a two-part company, one based on the Royal Opera House, Covent Garden, one on tour most of its time. This immense organization — there is also a flourishing school — was built up by Dame Ninette de Valois and is now directed by Sir Frederick Ashton. From the Royal Ballet you are sure of a high standard of professional excellence.

The other large company is London's Festival Ballet, which gets a good deal of publicity and attracts many people who do not go regularly to ballet as well as a very regular and loyal audience of its own. It is run by Dr. Julian Braunschweg, and its artistic director is John Gilpin.

Ballet Rambert, founded by Dame Marie Rambert, is not quite the magnificent cradle for talent that it once was — Antony Tudor and Frederick Ashton both started there; but it is still a company to reckon with; and interesting work has been done by other small companies such as Western Theatre Ballet, founded by the late Elizabeth West and directed by Peter Darrell, and the recently formed London Dance Theatre. Never write off a small company as unimportant — a good deal of the most exciting work in ballet has come from small companies.

There can be other differences in classical ballet, but most of them are not easily recognizable to the audience. Often you can see that one dancer holds her hands and arms differently from another, or has some other variation in style. This is probably due to a different method in training. But it is not really possible for us to place this without hesitation, as another dancer or a teacher would be able to do. And in fact it doesn't really matter very much to the onlooker at all.

When you have seen a fair number of companies and a good many other styles of dancing you begin, almost unconsciously, to have standards for ballet, and you apply them to every new ballet or company you see. All the same, one has to be careful.

My first experience of ballet was with Russian companies at big theatres. I loved every minute of it; and when I went to see companies at smaller theatres I went in a very superior frame of mind, convinced that they couldn't be much good. But of course I discovered that each company had its own character and its own good dancers and interesting ballets.

So try everything. Go and see ballet out of doors, even, if that is near you. Probably it will not be very successful — ballet is not in its element outside. It needs stage lighting, and the separation of stage and audience by an

Spanish Dance: Antonio

orchestra pit. Without that the magic is lost, the dancing seems only a physical exercise and the mime looks exaggerated. But it will all help you to think about ballet.

An excellent antidote for the times when you have been seeing too *much* classical ballet, and perhaps getting stale, is to go and look at other kinds of dancing. You may not like them all, but you are almost bound to find one type at least that you like a lot, because there are plenty of different forms of ballet. Some are very nearly what people think of as ballet, although from a technical point of view they may be quite unlike *classical* ballet. In this group have been various companies from Central Europe and the United States, such as the Ballets Jooss and the Martha Graham Dance Company. Most countries and races have dance companies and traditions. Sometimes they are in addition to classical ballet companies, like the national dance companies of Yugoslavia or Hungary or Poland — or the U.S.S.R. where, for instance, you get Cossack and other regional groups as well as the Bolshoi or Kirov Ballet. But in some parts of the world there is no Western classical ballet, only an individual and highly interesting national tradition, such as in the Spanish or Indian ballet companies.

Almost the only European country to have its own form of ballet and no important classical ballet companies is Spain, and quite a few companies of Spanish dancers go on tour. Probably the best-known is Antonio. In him you find all the characteristic fire, the brilliant timing and footwork, the energy and exuberance, the passion and

Indian Dance: Ram Gopal

drama of the Spanish dance at its best. But there are other dance groups than his, such as those of Pilar Lopez, Luisillo, and José Greco, and each one has his own particular excellences. Spanish dances fall into three main groups. There are the dances of the court and the nobility; there are the peasant dances from the different regions, among which are the various *jotas,* quick, gay dances; and there are the gypsy, or *flamenco,* dances which include the *zapateado,* the dance of the wonderful tapping footwork. Most of the Spanish companies give short ballets based on these forms of dancing, and *divertissements* made up of individual dances. Some of them are highly dramatic — José Greco has a ballet based on *Carmen* which compares most interestingly with Roland Petit's classical ballet on the same theme, or of course with Bizet's opera. Some of the dances are humorous ones, and Luisillo is particularly good at portraying a charming "witless countryman" in peasant sketches.

Many of our other visiting companies are from Asia. The form of Asian dancing most seen perhaps is the Indian. Uday Shankar, so famous before World War II, toured again not so long ago, and another well known name is Ram Gopal. All foreign dance companies have their own types of music and musicians. The Spanish dancers have guitars and castanets as accompaniment; the Asian dancers have many instruments strange to us and sometimes at first acquaintance rather comical, both in appearance and sound. But you get used to them, and they can in fact be very fascinating. There are drums and flutes and bells and many related instruments with native names and individual possibilities. Just as the Spanish dancer often wears and uses castanets, so the Indian dancer frequently has anklets of bells that make their own contribution to the musical accompaniment. Frequently — but not always; for Indian dancing has a very highly developed technique and is governed by many rules based on tradition; and only certain dances call for an accompaniment of bells.

In India there are six traditions of dance. There is the ancient temple dance, the Bharata Natyam, for Indian dancing has strong religious links; there is the Kathakali dance drama of Malabar; the Manipuri dance, which is often flowing and lyrical; the Kathak dance, where there is more stress on footwork; and the less known Odissi and Kuchipudi; while Indian mime is a complicated and endlessly fascinating language, based on hand movements called *mudras*.

It is very difficult for any foreigner to be more than just acquainted with the Indian dance. It is so complex, so much a world of its own, that we are very much outsiders, understanding only as it were one word in ten. But most Indian dancers act as interpreters to us, for they frequently explain what they are doing and tell us the meaning of various *mudras* so that when next we see one of the dances we understand much more.

The Indian dance is rich in color — magnificent costumes, gold adorned, headdresses and necklets and bracelets for men and women; it is rich in intoxicating movement, and it is rich in significance. One dancer can create a landscape. There is a Kathakali dance where a young

Indian walks in a garden. It is spring. He comes to the river, he washes his face and arms; he catches a bird which flutters away from him, he gathers flowers and makes a garland. All this, on a bare stage, comes as much alive as though you could hear the splash of water, the singing of birds, and smell the scent of the flowers. The whole natural world can be expressed in Indian dance. There are magnificent dances based on the movements of birds or reptiles, like the Cobra Devil Dance where the dancer is possessed by the spirit of a cobra, or Garuda the Golden Eagle, where the strong slow beat of the great golden wings is hypnotic in its beauty.

But not only the natural world provides subjects, and some of the dances which are most impressive are religious in origin. They cannot be described so easily, but their impact is tremendous, such as the clear tranquillity of the Deevali Puja, the ritual dance celebrating the Festival of Light, in which a white-clad youth carries the lighted lamps into a shrine; or the majestic modern Dance of the Setting Sun in which the dancer is the Lord Siva high on the peaks of the Himalayas.

Indian dancing is, however, only one of many forms of Asian dancing, although one of the oldest. There have been exciting seasons by Balinese dancers, or the famous Japanese Azuma Kabuki, who perform dance-dramas blending song, dance and mime. The Philippine Islanders recently exported their Bayanihan Company and showed an extremely interesting range of dances. Some of them were primitive pictures of war and victory and weddings; some were strongly influenced by their Spanish conquerors; some from various regions, including a fascinating dance where the dancers step in and out of sets of bamboo poles which are clapped together in rapid rhythms; and some that show a Middle Eastern Muslim influence.

One of the Asian companies most delightful to watch was the Classical Theatre of China. This is not, in fact, a ballet company: its members are at one and the same time singers, actors and dancers — they present long dramas which are a mixture of opera, play and ballet. But many of the episodes they showed us could be termed dance-dramas, as they depended for their effect largely on movement and mime to music. They combined drama and comedy, expert mime, marvelous split-second timing and acrobatic feats, with rich costume and ornament. One of them was called *Where Three Roads Meet* and was about a wicked innkeeper and his wife who decided to kill and rob an army officer and his escort. There was a hilarious scene in this when (on a fully lit stage) the innkeeper entered what to him was supposed to be a dark bedroom and had a fight with the army officer. Both were supposed to be slashing at each other in the dark, and the expert timing of their movements made it completely convincing that they couldn't see each other, though *we* could see them both. Then there was the scene called *Autumn River,* when a lady (played, as is their tradition, by a man) comes to a river and wishes to board a boat punted by an old man. Here too the action, which is all make-believe, bears absolute conviction,

Chinese Dance: The Monkey King

and you are never in doubt for a moment as to what is happening or which is dry land and which the river.

The Middle East sends out companies more rarely, but we *have* seen the National Ballet of Israel, Inbal, which has its unique and interesting methods of expression. From Mexico comes the brilliant color and vitality of the Ballet Folklorico. All these and others offer a stimulating contrast to classical ballet, just as do such groups as the Ballets Jooss and the Martha Graham Dance Company. The Ballets Jooss developed out of what is called the Central European dance movement of the 1920's, and was founded by Kurt Jooss in 1932. The ballets which were most famous in this company were *The Green Table,* which was about war and peace conferences and refugees; and *The Big City,* which reflected contemporary city life. In a similar way Martha Graham and her company have made an important contribution to ballet, because ballet is by no means limited to Western classical ballet. The style of dancing she employs is not classical ballet, but it needs very highly trained dancers and can achieve a very impressive effect.

All these other forms are there to see, to appreciate, and to learn from. The important point with them all is that you must be *ready* to appreciate them and enjoy them. They will often seem very strange and different to you, but that is their great value. *All* differences in life are valuable. So do not limit yourself to classical ballet; look about you and see all the rest the world has to offer in the way of ballet and the dance, and you will find each will sharpen the impact of the other.

Different kinds of ballet

Every balletgoer comes up against all kinds of "extensions" of the ballet. Over and above the regular companies from all over the world and their repertoires, there are various "fringe" activities, some of them of considerable interest.

There is ballet in opera. This varies from the odd —
sometimes *very* odd — short dance for two or three couples to the complete *scène de ballet*. There are plenty of examples of the latter. There is the Venusberg scene in *Tannhäuser;* there is the ballet in *Faust* (a version of which was filmed by the Bolshoi Ballet) ; there are the Polovtsian Dances in *Prince Igor* — and they, of course, have been part of the regular ballet repertory; there is the circus scene in *The Bartered Bride,* and quite a few others.

Sometimes an opera company has only a little team of dancers attached to it, but most of the important opera houses have their own ballet companies to draw on often with world-famous dancers as *maîtres de ballet*. Dame Alicia Markova, for instance, is in charge of ballet at the Metropolitan Opera House, New York. They can have choreography by topline choreographers, often danced by accomplished soloists. But in most opera houses, however hard the directors of ballet work, opera still naturally comes first and ballet a very poor second. Only at Covent Garden and in Copenhagen are the ballet companies of equal or greater importance. In Russian opera houses, opera and ballet share the stage equally.

Some of the best known choreographers of our time have directed operas, and occasionally there are mimed parts in opera which are taken by dancers.

It is always worthwhile therefore to check up on the opera repertoire, on light opera, to watch the concert list for the occasional *pas de deux* or dance recital, and of course to keep an eye on musical plays generally. All musical plays probably have some dancing, even if it is rarely classical ballet. If it *is* classical ballet it is often second-rate. Even a first-rate choreographer cannot really deliver a first-rate classical ballet in a musical play, for various reasons. Very often the management does not engage a first-rate team of classical dancers — they are usually dancers who are primarily skilled in putting over "modern dance" and only secondarily classical dancers; very often there is not a sufficiently strict ballet mistress to keep them up to standard technically through a long run; always there is the deadening influence of doing the same show evening after evening, sometimes twice a day, without any of the variety offered by a ballet repertoire. If the show is on tour the dancers may have difficulty finding the right sort of classes to go to — you will remember all dancers have to have class every day. Then, a ballet in a musical play usually has to aim at immediate effect and it usually has to be composed to second-rate music — second-rate, I mean, from the point of view of classical ballet! It has to contend, too, with an audience that is not used to classical ballet, and is often unreceptive to the point of stupid giggling. Not long ago I found myself in such an audience, where the very sight of a girl

Ballet in Opera: Die Fledermaus *(Metropolitan Opera House, New York)*

in a draped, gauzy costume and a man in tights and tunic convulsed my neighbors. It took me about five minutes to work out what was amusing them. . . .

The strong card of the musical play is of course the type of ballet that came to full flower in *West Side Story*. This dancing, springing from classical ballet sources but adapted to the contemporary mood, is acceptable to the non-ballet audience. It is a progression, in some ways, from the dance sequences in the Astaire-Rogers films of the 1930's. It has their young exuberance, their sinuous and supple movement. It lacks their polish and unforgettable superb timing (did you ever see a revival of, say, *Follow the Fleet?*). But it expresses, in a way that everyone accepts, the current attitude to the theatre: rather down-to-earth, in that there is nothing romantic about the characters — they are sidewalk and coffee-bar types; rather violent and sexy, because fights and love and lust are all popular subjects nowadays; rather sentimental, because that has always an appeal for the public; rather influenced by psychological doctrines but never supplying very much to think about. American musicals lead the world for the vitality of their dance numbers. Agnes De Mille was a pioneer with *Oklahoma* and today some of the best known names in musicals are Hanya Holm, Michael Kidd, Gower Champion, Bob Fosse and Joe Layton.

It is always difficult to define the differences between ballet proper — that is, ballets given by a regular ballet company — and other outcroppings of ballet. Sometimes they are so much alike that it is largely by a kind of instinct that you can decide which category a ballet comes

Ballet in Musicals: West Side Story

Martha Graham and Paul Taylor in **Clytemnestra** *(Martha Graham Dance Company)*

into. Earlier in this book I quoted Noverre's warning about ballets where "dancing was introduced for the sake of dancing." But that needs to be made clearer. It does not mean ballets like *Les Sylphides* or, for example, Balanchine's *Four Temperaments*. There, dancing is not introduced "for the sake of dancing" but for the sake of projecting a certain kind of mood or sequence of moods in reflecting the changing moods of the music. The type of thing I think Noverre was tilting at is approached in, for instance, the "divertissement" acts of *The Sleeping Beauty* or *Coppélia* — legitimate when they are given the slight excuse of a celebration at the end of a story: wedding festivities for Florimund and Aurora, or a village festival in *Coppélia,* because then they are part of something that certainly is a ballet; but not really legitimate when they are done on their own without being led up to by the rest of the action, because then they are *simply* "dancing introduced for the sake of dancing."

I think Noverre's reservations about this spring from the fact that there is actually a very thin line in ballet between an artistic presentation of dancing, and a show, or acrobatic, or music hall, or circus presentation of it. Audiences have always loved spectacular ballets, and it is an ever-recurring danger that they will, by their enthusiasm, push ballet towards the spectacular divertissement at the cost of the more serious and less showy works. When Benjamin Lumley, manager of Covent Garden in the nineteenth century, wrote his reminiscences he said about the audience: "They wanted only dancing, not acting, they said. They should, to tell the truth, have

said 'We only want legs, not brains.' " This is the same
danger that Noverre was worried about in the previous
century. It is difficult to be quite clear on this point, but
let us take examples. At one extreme, say, is a ballet like
Giselle — a dramatic, tragic story that needs fine dancing
and acting, and can only be accepted by an audience that
is prepared to watch pure ballet and appreciate fine dancing and acting. At the other extreme you have, say, a pair
of specialty dancers, who dance a *pas de deux* partly de-
rived from classical ballet technique and partly from
acrobatic technique, put together and performed purely
as a spectacle, as something for people to look at while
they sit and have supper or take a rest from ballroom
dancing themselves. In these two cases there are three
main differences. The purpose of the dancing is different: in the first case, it is the same purpose as a play — to
captivate the audience by the story and make them feel
for the situations and characters and think about what is
going on; in the second case, merely to give them something to look at to pass the time. The performance is
different: in the first case, the dancers are expressing
characters and moods and emotions, they are sharing an
experience with the audience, and they are taking care to
keep their standards of dancing and acting as high as they
possibly can without letting in the slightest degree of
showmanship; whereas in the second case the performance is intended to be showy, to be spectacular, to echo
the spangled tightrope walkers and bareback riders of

the circus and live up to a cracking of whips by a ring-master.

Finally, the attitude of the audience is different: in the first case the audience has come for no other reason than to watch the ballet, to see the story unfold before it in terms of beautiful movement and expressive mime; it will follow it with attention and look on it as an artistic experience. In the second case the audience will look at the dancing idly, it will chat and eat and drink if it feels like it and it will dismiss it from its mind as soon as it is over.

These two examples are well defined. But not all ballets are of the unspectacular nature of *Giselle,* and not all spectacular dancing is as blatant as the night club *duo.* So you get a point somewhere in the middle where there are two ballets, both full of technical brilliance and spectacular elements, and it is at that point that you need an extra sense to be able to say which of them qualifies to be regarded as a ballet in the artistic sense, and which of them slips over the line into the world of the ballet fringe, the dance scene in a musical play or revue.

I cannot give you real guidance on this. In some cases, even, you will see a ballet in a musical play which you can easily imagine becoming part of the repertoire of a regular ballet company; and in some cases, watching a ballet company, you may find yourself thinking of some work, "It doesn't really belong in the ballet repertoire." But mostly you will be in very little doubt, even if you cannot put your reasons into words.

CINEMA AND TELEVISION

There are two ways now by which more people see ballet than ever before: cinema and television — but what they see is not always ballet at its most enchanting.

Of course there are various kinds of films about ballet.

The first ballet film I remember seeing was long ago, in 1938. It was French and it was called *La Mort du Cygne* (*Ballerina* in the U.S.). It had a rather melodramatic story — ballet films tend to, one finds — about rivalries at the Paris Opéra. One of the little girls at the ballet school tremendously admires a particular ballerina in the company and is jealous on her account of her rival. Without realizing the harm she is doing she crawls under the stage and opens up a trapdoor. The rival falls down while she is dancing *La Mort du Cygne* and injures her leg so badly that she is crippled for life. She becomes a teacher in the school and when she discovers that the little girl was responsible she is, naturally, bitterly resentful; but in the end they come to a better understanding.

Now this story, like the one used some ten years later for *The Red Shoes,* is improbable nonsense. But *La Mort du Cygne* was all the same very memorable. I can remember the most imaginative black and white photography of the ballet school, the backstage scenes and even, to a lesser degree, the performances. The three chief characters were drawn from the Paris Opéra Ballet itself. Yvette Chauviré and a Yugoslavian ballerina, Mia Slavenska, were the rival dancers, and the little girl was quite beautifully played by Janine Charrat who is now well-known in French ballet both for dancing and choreography.

The Red Shoes, a British film, to some extent had a similar pattern. At least it had its unbelievable central story, this time about a ballerina who was so torn between her profession and her married life that she threw herself in front of a train to resolve the problem; and it had its professional ballet stars in Moira Shearer, Robert Helpmann and Leonide Massine. Once again there was some exciting photography, particularly in the ballet which brought the heroine fame, the ballet of *The Red Shoes.* In *La Mort du Cygne* the interest chiefly rested in the backstage sequences; in *The Red Shoes* chiefly in the specially created ballet. The backstage atmosphere in *The Red Shoes* was an odd mixture — in some ways real enough, but glossed over with a false varnish. That wild rush of audience into the Covent Garden gallery, for instance, at the beginning, taken at impossible speed and force: it looked completely phony; because you get into the gallery at Covent Garden by an elaborate system of lining up on the day of booking, in order to get a special ticket to enable you to get back later in the day and book your theatre tickets. . . . All the same, in prewar days people did wait outside in a line on the day of performance and rush up the stairs (perhaps not quite so fast!) to make sure of a good place inside, just as they did in most theatre galleries, which were all unreserved. No, *The Red Shoes* was not all basically false — but film commercialism gave it all a heightened color that falsified its truth.

From the point of view of a good film, the impossibilities in the stories of *La Mort du Cygne* and *The Red Shoes* rule them both out. You cannot credit that a pupil of an opera house ballet school could for one moment think that it was not a colossally dangerous thing to open a trapdoor on stage. The little girl, living in a theatre atmosphere, would be well aware of what she was doing, and she wouldn't do it! In the same way there was no justification for the girl in *The Red Shoes* to kill herself so dramatically. But if neither film was particularly good from the point of view of fine works of cinema art, both are interesting if you are interested in ballet. *Ballerina,* alas, has been withdrawn from general circulation.

If you get a chance to see any ballet films of this kind, don't dismiss them entirely because of their impossibilities, nor because of their often very bad dialogue, nor even because they are tainted with the layman's firm belief that ballet is a terribly intense, emotional, personal, melodramatic kind of art. This belief began because the first people to tour widely with a ballet company were the Diaghilev Ballet. They were a mixture of races, mainly Russian and Polish, with a dash of various other nationalities. To the minds of many who had a chance of seeing them off stage they seemed extremely emotional and melodramatic; but that was not so much because they were ballet dancers as because they were Slavs.

There are other types of ballet films than the ones which have a story mixed up in them. There are "educational" or "documentary" ones. You sometimes find a program that includes films on various types of dancing. I remember one that had a fascinating documentary about Indian dancing called *Lord Siva Dances,* with a commentary by Ram Gopal. It was followed by the English *Steps of the Ballet* showing how a short classical ballet is rehearsed and put on; and then there were some short films of Soviet folk dancing and classical ballet to finish up with. Every now and then you will see a notice of a new film in this category — Martha Graham made an exciting one not long ago called *A Dancer's World* — and it is a good way to get acquainted with forms of dancing you may not have the chance to see on stage. Then there are the films of ballets which are in the theatre repertoires of the major companies. The most publicized ones of the kind have been those of the Bolshoi Ballet and the Royal Ballet. I think, after seeing these, you may well decide that they miss the real charm and fascination of ballet in the theatre. But they are splendid for people who cannot get to the theatre — and there are lots of those in the world. In fact, they may well be a revelation to plenty who have never had the opportunity of seeing these great companies in actual fact.

If you have seen the Bolshoi and Royal Ballet films, you will be very conscious by the end that there is nothing *real* about them. Ballet, even in the theatre, has a quality of unreality; but in the theatre it is danced by real people. They are there, in the flesh, before you on the stage. There is the exciting feeling that this particular performance has never happened before. It is all being freshly done for you that evening — no one at all knows what is to happen.

To take an example. However often one went, say, to

the Royal Ballet film's *Ondine* it would of course each time be exactly the same. But any ballet you saw an equivalent (or greater) number of times on stage would be different each one of those times. Perhaps that night a new principal dancer would be tried out; perhaps the choreographer would have a new idea for some small point; perhaps a piece of the scenery would stick; perhaps someone would fall over. Whatever it was, there would be a difference. And that makes it real, because real life never exactly repeats itself. So the film, any film, is quite unreal; and because there is already an unreality about ballet, a film of a ballet never, I think, captures an audience as does a ballet performance on stage.

There are all sorts of other points. Great dancers do not always photograph well. Neither Ulanova nor Fonteyn has been seen to really good advantage on their films. Some of their quality as dancers certainly is captured — enough to show how really great they both are — but that is not enough.

However, it is easy enough to pick holes in films of ballets. You must see them for yourself, because whatever you think, anyone who is interested in ballet must take an interest in ballet films. Probably, too, we all secretly long for a film recording of some ballet or performance that has completely captivated us. Memory is not sufficiently strong or photographic to preserve things perfectly. But we should of course simply want a record: no special angles, or selections made by the cameraman — just an absolute record of what happened on the entire stage that time, so that we could see it again whenever we wanted.

It is the element of record that makes historic films nostalgic and fascinating. There is one of Pavlova, including scraps of her dances: poignant and moving in *The Dying Swan*, warm and gay in *Christmas*; and although it is an unpretentious record, made on the spur of a moment in Hollywood by Douglas Fairbanks Senior, it still holds something, some quality, that makes those of us who never saw her more able to believe in the tales we have heard of her magic.

Of course where the cinema has traveled away from the idea of simply filming a classical ballet it has often been completely successful. Fred Astaire's films have shown what a magnificent effect dance scenes can have on the screen, and Astaire, in line, in timing and in expressive movement, is a major artist of the dance. Gene Kelly's films, like *An American in Paris*, have continued the tradition, and Jerome Robbins' *West Side Story* had an immediate success; all these show how necessary it is to adapt ballet to the film medium rather than for the cinema to adapt itself to the classical ballet. It seems to me that, in the matter of success, films of existing ballets like *Giselle* or *Ondine* (for all their merits) have less vitality and reality than, for all their faults, films of specially composed ballets like Roland Petit's *Little Mermaid* (in *Hans Christian Andersen*) or Helpmann's *Red Shoes*; and that dance scenes of the Astaire/Kelly variety are superior again. But ballet films are still being made or projected and perhaps one of them will manage to shift the balance in my opinion. . . .

One last point: by some curious twist ballet, which is

Dancing in Films: Cyd Charisse and Fred Astaire in Silk Stockings

so dependent on color in the theatre, seems over-colored on the screen. Coming away from the Royal Ballet film, for instance, I felt exhausted by watching color — a feeling you never get from a stage, probably because of the third dimension of depth. There seemed far too much of it — and yet one revels in color in the theatre.

Television too has the problem of whether to televise ballets out of the theatre repertoire, or ballets specially composed for the medium. It does both, and some of the occasions when it has televised theatre ballets it has been successful. Its most complete successes have been, I think, in the small-scale ballet for a handful of dancers, and in the various *pas de deux* which are done from time to time. The Royal Ballet's *Sleeping Beauty* and, to a lesser extent, *Cinderella,* made history when shown on American television but, alas, did not establish a precedent.

The majority of ballets depend, to a very large extent, on one's usual ability to see the whole of a full-size stage — to get the proper sweep of *corps-de-ballet* dancing, or the full circle of *pirouettes* and *jetés*; clever camera angles, sudden close-ups, shifting lines of vision all destroy the essential structure of the ballet as composed for the theatre, where the sequence of action and of dancing has been created for an audience who can see it all, but at a distance. The mad scene in *Giselle,* for example, as we watch it in the theatre, could only be shown on the screen as a distant shot, too small and dull to have any interest. It has to be brought nearer the viewer by close-ups of Giselle or Albrecht or some of the other characters. But the full effect of that scene, as watched in the theatre, is brought

Making the Royal Ballet Film: Margot Fonteyn in The Firebird

about by a combination of factors: by the performances of Giselle and Albrecht certainly — and probably we are constantly switching from one to the other to register the full tragedy; and also by the secondary, but important, reactions from the minor characters, like Giselle's mother; and by the half circle of shocked and anxious peasants and court attendants.

In the theatre all this is in front of us all the time; we may watch one thing in particular, but we are still conscious of the full scene and it is the full scene that is really making the effect as much as the single dancer we may be looking at. So the television cameras cannot, on a small screen, bring that full effect into being. I don't know if televised performances of ballets from the theatre repertoire make many people interested in ballet if they are not so already; but I am pretty certain that they can never really satisfy anyone who can see the stage performances.

They are of course better than nothing. They make up a little for people who love ballet but cannot easily get to the theatre. But there is more satisfaction in a really good dance scene specially composed for television. Television has, after all, much the same wide audience as the musical play, and so it is with "modern dance" rather than classical ballet that it is most at home.

Ballet on TV: Nadia Nerina and Robert Helpmann in Coppélia

PART FOUR

Sharing the ballet

PART FOUR
SHARING THE BALLET

One of the things you need above all others if you are really going to get fun out of ballet as a hobby is to know people who are also interested in it.

Friends are tremendously important. Now it is not a good idea to try to limit your friends to the people who have exactly the same interests as yourself. Speaking for myself (and that's the only way anyone can speak), one of the nicest facts about my life is that I have friends who do all kinds of jobs, from painting pictures to driving people on bus trips, and who live in all parts of the world and have all kinds of different enthusiasms. Their experience adds to my own and makes life a lot more interesting.

All the same, you do need friends who share your own interests too. And if ballet is one of these, you need people who can agree with you or argue with you, or just sit for hours on end exchanging news and views about what you have all seen and done.

How do you get these friends — particularly if you do

not start off with anyone who is as interested as you are in ballet?

Well, there are more orthodox ways — but I found most of mine by meeting them in theatres or buying tickets (of course you can find your *bêtes noires* that way too!). If you go regularly to performances you begin to see the same people over and over again, and perhaps chance throws you together with one or two in particular, or you realize you share some special admiration for a ballet or a dancer, or you just like the look of one another; and the friendship gradually emerges. There is a lot of good fortune about the making of friends in every part of one's life; and perhaps the only advice one person can ever give another is to be receptive and to grasp an opportunity.

You may perhaps find your opportunity through your nearest regional ballet company, if you do not live in New York. This is one of the principal ways in which the art of ballet is being fostered in the U.S.A., for regional ballet companies encourage a great deal of talent that would not otherwise find an outlet, and help to fill in the gaps of the year when none of the touring or visiting ballet companies have dates in the neighborhood.

Admittedly, regional ballet companies have more facilities for people who want to dance or try choreography than for those who want to learn about ballet or talk about ballet. They probably think of the audience more in its character of people who pay to watch performances than as people who want to contribute their share of alert intelligent appreciation and criticism. All the same, you may find a place as a non-dancer, helping perhaps with making costumes, scene-painting, or some other backstage job, and so make friends with the same interests with whom you can discuss ballet. Alternatively, you can join the ballet society or guild which most companies have, by paying a small fee every year. That way you can help your local company financially, and the fee usually includes privileges — the chance of attending rehearsals, special "get together" parties, and occasionally lecture-demonstrations or showings of dance films. The New York Ballet Club is especially active, with monthly talks from well-known dance personalities. Some colleges give lectures in dance history, but these are rarely available except to full-time students.

Keep a lookout in your local newspaper, in *Dance News* or *Dance Magazine*, for announcements of any activities which may be fruitful for you: talks — talks may sound dull but it is surprising how interesting they can be and often how amusing; lecture-demonstrations — they are always fascinating, whether they are on a subject of great general importance to ballet, like mime, or a very specialized part of it, like historical dance; film shows — and there are plenty of dance films which might appear in programs arranged by schools or colleges or libraries; exhibitions, of photographs or paintings or books. Your library might help in putting you on to this kind of thing, if they knew you were interested.

COLLECTING MATERIAL

Now all the time you are going to performances, to lectures and film shows and classes, you are probably piling up at home quite extensive collections of stuff about ballet. By stuff — rather an irreverent word — I mean you have probably got quite a bundle of programs and souvenir books and possibly magazines like *Dance News* or *Dance Magazine* and press clippings — notices of performances or news pictures or gossip bits about dancers. You may have acquired some actual photographs. Anyway, all this may be stacked up in some cupboard and quite possibly it is in the kind of state when you can't find anything you want to look up anyway, without delving down to the bottom of the pile.

Now it depends very much on whether you have any fancy for keeping things straight whether you try to organize your own "special collection."

I wonder if it ever occurred to you that actually all this type of material — the programs and souvenir books, the press clippings and photographs — is really the documentation from which the story of ballet is written? How do ballet historians work? Well, they go to the big libraries like the New York Public Library or the Reading Room at the British Museum in London where they can look up rare books, or turn the pages of newspapers right back to the eighteenth century. They usually have to get a special ticket to do this. It is an entrancing occupation. It can be exhausting — you have to look through a lot of newspapers, for instance, to get just the one kind of fact you want. But it gives you, as a sideline, a wonderful bird's-eye view of another age. There are advertisements for houses, and medical cures, and books; there are accounts of great events, and of murders, and of scandals, as well as the theatre news. You get very sidetracked, sometimes. . . .

Most of the important theatres, like the opera houses, have their own museums where you can find musical scores and playbills and relics of various sorts, and there are other specialist collections you get to know about. But the point is that all these collections are based on just the sort of thing we ourselves collect as members of the audience — first-night programs, notices and news reports, and photographs and books.

These big collections can usually produce any item that is asked for, and ours could too. After all, not much is needed in the way of outlay — you really only need to think straight, and try to get into a habit of putting things away systematically. And you can work out your own system. This can be extremely simple. You can just put all the programs, company by company, in boxes in date order. You can keep the photographs in separate polythene folders (bought at any office supply store) for different ballets and put the whole lot in box files; and you can paste your news clippings into scrapbooks or simply store them in polythene bags. Newspaper clippings, however, go brown with the years unless they are mounted. None of that is hard to do and in fact it can be a rather pleasant occupation for winter evenings. . . . But some enthusiasts I know are much more ambitious. They have card index

systems and keep cross-records of ballets and dancers they
have seen and so on. You may be one of these — in which
case you will work out your own ideas without any more
words on the subject!

My own accumulation of material has been a source of
pleasure, and of course, problems over the years. It
mounts up surprisingly. But it is interesting to turn up
clippings of half-forgotten seasons, and read references to
ballets you either loved or hated in the past. The real fun,
however, has lain in the collecting. Thinking of that, I
remember plenty of calls at photographers and newspaper
offices; interviews with every sort of custodian of papers
and photographs from office boys to Great Men of Photography; the difficulty of ordering prints from negatives
on which you can never see facial expressions; the anxiety
of finding you have been so carried away that you have
ordered more than you can really afford, and the consola-
tion of at least having the prints long after you have got
over the extravagance; the abortive attempts to get something out of a heavily regulated office with no idea of co-
operation; the really warm pleasant feeling when you find
yourself dealing with someone who is willing to be help-
ful and lets you search until you find what you want. Photographs and news clippings have led me to all sorts of
unexpected places, just as following ballet has led me to
theatres and halls of all descriptions. There have been
violent contrasts — from opera houses to church halls in
the suburbs, from modern concert halls to little old half-
forgotten theatres. I've watched ballet right through the
British Isles and everywhere else I have happened to

travel. That's the kind of hobby ballet can become — something that is part of your life, and that goes with you wherever *you* go.

There has been an audience for ballet for a very long time. On some occasions I have been very conscious myself of being part of a long story — for instance, when watching *Giselle* in the Paris Opera House, the theatre where it was first performed in 1841, I have realized that just as the dancers are keeping alive a tradition by dancing *Giselle* on that stage, I am keeping one alive by buying my ticket and sitting there on the other side of the footlights. They are a continuation of a line that began with Carlotta Grisi and Lucien Petipa, the first Giselle and Albrecht; *I* am in the direct line from the nineteenth-century audience; and I begin to try to imagine what that audience was like.

By the nineteenth century the audience would have lost the quality it once had of being drawn almost entirely from the nobility and the wealthy leisured classes. From the time of the French Revolution more "ordinary" people went to the ballet. But of course it was still the custom to wear very correct evening dress, at least in the more expensive seats. If you look up a book of costume through the ages you see the kind of gowns the women wore, the kind Queen Victoria wore as a young woman: low-necked, with tiny sleeves, crinolined skirts, long white gloves; they carried fans, and their hair was looped down on either side of a center parting and gathered into the nape of the neck. The Opera House tiers and boxes would have sparkled with the jeweled tiaras and necklaces and bracelets. But this audience was by no means too sophisticated and blasé to be excited. They were keenly interested in ballet and in the rival merits of all the dancers. They watched it through long-sticked lorgnettes, and opera glasses. Gautier, speaking of a farewell performance by Marie Taglioni in 1844, writes:

> All the opera-glasses are aimed and pointed at her, not those light opera-glasses which can be slipped into one's coat-pocket, but those large field glasses, those twin monsters, those optical mortars which will make the people of the future think we were a race of giants. . . .

One custom they had has died out. They took along posies and bouquets of flowers, and sat holding them (they must have wilted a little) through the evening so that "the circles resemble a flowermarket, so tightly massed are the bouquets." Then at the end they flung them onto the stage. We think now that a ballerina is well supplied when we see her coming forward after a ballet with both arms full of flowers, and flowers on the ground beside her in sheafs and baskets. But how does it compare with this? Taglioni in 1844 received "a shower of bouquets, a whirlwind of flowers. At one moment her life seemed to be in danger, so vigorous, intense and prolonged was the perfumed bombardment. The curtain was

Margot Fonteyn and Rudolf Nureyev in Swan Lake (Royal Ballet)

unable to descend, so thick was the carpet of roses, camellias and parma violets." Flowers still carpet the stage in some parts of the world, however, according to reports — in South America, for instance.

Flower throwing was the custom in Paris and London some time before it was introduced into Russia. But in St. Petersburg balletomanes were always in existence, and Karsavina describes them as "a very knowledgeable, exacting, somewhat dogmatic and conservative public" — a "regular" audience, in fact! They applauded from the stalls, they shouted from the gallery, and they waited at the stage door, like all other ballet enthusiasts. But some of them had excesses of devotion that have been smiled at ever since: balletomanes who had a ballerina's shoe cooked and served with a special sauce, and ate it; who drank champagne out of ballet slippers; who would eat nothing that was not served up on plates decorated with a design of dancers.

Flowers, of course, are given to men in Oriental countries, and you will see Indian male dancers presented with bouquets and garlands. Our Western convention runs to nothing more exciting for men than an occasional large and funereal-looking laurel wreath tied up with ribbon, like a memento propped against a cenotaph; a single flower, extracted from a ballerina's bouquet (more difficult now when so much is polythene wrapped), possibly kissed, and handed over as a thank offering for a partner's efforts; or a few flowers flung on stage by a determined fan.

Curtain calls have not really increased over the years.

We have plenty nowadays — but we do not often overtop Taglioni's twenty-two calls at Vienna — and that night the horses were taken out of her carriage and she was drawn triumphantly home to her hotel by a team of forty young noblemen. In international relations, ballet is now very much the thing: reciprocal visits are arranged, a great deal is said about dancing being a world language. An enthusiasm for ballet is one of the emotions that seem really identical on both sides of the Iron Curtain. All the same, I am not sure it has quite the place it had in 1845 when the *Pas de Quatre* danced in London by Taglioni, Grisi, Grahn and Cerito was described as "the one universal topic of the day. Even ambassadors described it at length in dispatches."

Throughout its career the ballet audience has always been the most vociferous in the theatre, and amused or disgusted people outside itself. Horace Walpole, the great English letter writer of the eighteenth century, has a nice "tongue-in-cheek" passage about a performance by the dancer Auguste Vestris: "The ladies clapped with such vehemence that 17 broke their arms, 69 sprained their wrists, and three cried Bravo, Bravissimo so rashly that they have not been able to utter so much as No since." In our time there have been plenty of written and spoken digs at ecstatic audiences — and it is true of course that ballet always promotes a far more excited reception than a straight play. The finest acted Hamlet or Othello will get only a small proportion of the reception expended on a performance of, say, the Bluebird *pas de deux*.

A custom that has largely died out — and a good thing

too — is the encore. It used to be quite usual, in the nineteenth century, for a popular variation to be repeated when the audience shouted for an encore. In the ballet *Paquita*, for instance, a dance was encored twice after the fall of the curtain. Gautier — how invaluable he is as a recorder of the audience as well as the dancer — deplored the habit. He "quite understood the desire to have a second view of something that has delighted one — but then we should book a box or stall for the morrow and come back"; it was "somewhat mean and sordid" to want to "see the same thing twice for the one payment." I think under most circumstances his argument is absolutely valid. To encore dances is to reduce their effect very dangerously — and to do it regularly would drive some people (including me) out of the theatre. Outside classical ballet it is, however, slightly different; the encored finales of Spanish dance companies are, for instance, very much a tradition.

Another lost — and properly lost — custom is that of the audience sitting on the stage. This theatrical tradition goes very far back — it was prevailing at Shakespeare's Globe and it comes right down the years to the eighteenth century. There was a benefit performance for Auguste Vestris in 1781 (and benefits for individual artists, who received all the proceeds of that performance, have died out as well), when the house was so crowded that even after a delay of two hours, while the audience and the management argued, the ballet only got under way with a hundred and fifty people seated on a platform at the back of the stage and at both sides as well.

Audiences like and dislike, they make and break, they laugh and weep, they boo and bravo. They follow the same pattern across the world and through the years. They have their favorites, they send flowers, they write letters (to dancers, to managements and to the press), they wait at stage doors, they ask for autographs (autograph books are a relatively recent development). They are sometimes fickle — the public that had loved Fanny Cerito is recorded as later being "bored with her talent and all the bravos are now given to Saint Leon." They are often faithful, and welcome back dancers after long intervals with warmth and affection. They have their great moments in the theatre, and they have their shocks, their excitements, their accidents and tragedies.

The tragedies have been such occasions as the on-stage fires which fatally injured Emma Livry in Paris or Clara Webster in London during the nineteenth century. But there have been plenty of accidents that have not proved tragic or fatal. Arnold Haskell, in *Balletomania*, recalls an exciting occasion when the dancer Rostova came rushing on stage during Act II of *Swan Lake* with her clothes on fire; but that fire was extinguished in time. There was the time when Zizi Jeanmaire was accidentally stabbed in the arm during *Carmen*; when Melissa Hayden fell and stunned herself during *The Duel* and the curtain was lowered for a few minutes until she recovered; the time, back in 1838, when in *La Sylphide* the pulleys stuck and two sylphs were suspended in mid-air. "People in the audience cried out in terror" but the girls were brought down safely. There was the time in 1849 when a dancer called

Mlle. Maria pirouetted too near the open footlights, saw her danger from fire, and leapt over them to land on the shoulders of a member of the orchestra. There have been any number of sprained ankles, torn ligaments, accidental blows during *pas de deux*, scratches from costume ornaments and so on; and you can lose count of the number of times when, for one reason or another, you experience that always-chilling moment when a dancer crumples and falls.

It is usually followed, of course, by a quick recovery. Sometimes it can even fool most people into thinking it was intentional. There was a charming occasion some years ago when on the first night of a new ballet a leading dancer slipped and fell and recovered; and a critic later complimented her on the clever *intentional* slip. . . .

Dancers are very good at coping with emergencies, and most audiences treasure memories of well-dealt-with situations. For instance, I have seen a good many costumes come to pieces on stage. A dancer in the last act of *Coppélia* lost her skirt; she kicked it aside and went on dancing in the short basque. A peasant girl soloist in Act I of *Swan Lake* finished her dance with only one shoe. The ribbon-trimming on a Swanilda's last act costume caught on the wings and unwrapped itself as she pirouetted. The light layers of a Giselle's second-act costume came away one after the other in her partner's hands (not, fortunately, the final one!) and he had to dispose of them unobtrusively, into the wings, behind the cross, tucked into his own tunic. . . . Curtains come up or go down in the wrong places and stage tricks refuse to function. I have even seen a performance when the stage and orchestra pit lights failed and a ballet was played by the orchestra in semi-darkness and danced to one spotlight on the stage.

Perhaps above all there are two moments when dancers and audience are bound together more firmly than at any other: for the début of a dancer, and at a farewell performance. A début can be very exciting and very touching, when a young dancer dances a famous role for the first time, emerging as a new Swan Queen or Giselle or Aurora, offering her new personality to the age-long series of interpretations that stretches back into the past. For the farewell performance let Gautier speak, in his sensitive nineteenth-century style: "When the curtain falls on the conclusion, one experiences the same sort of sadness which is felt on seeing a post-chaise carry away one's beloved. The first turn of the wheel is over one's heart. . . ."

This, then, is the job you take on if you become a serious balletgoer: the job of making up the audience, of being one of the two halves that equal the art of ballet. You will have many different relationships with the dancers: the student, the critic, the entertained, the defender, the supporter, the friend, the partner. You will need to provide thought and understanding, enthusiasm and love; and to love an art, just as to love a person, is something that involves you in every sort of contrasted reaction: in confidence and anxiety, in elation and disappointment, in sorrow and in great happiness. All the same, you are never likely to regret it. Ballet, like every other art, is capable of rewarding magnificently those who devote themselves to it. Moreover it will, if you let it, push your knowledge and interests outward to embrace the associated arts of music and painting and drama, so that your life and mind are enriched. And if that sounds rather a dull and prosy sort of consequence, I can only say try it, and see. . . .

178

Bibliography

BIBLIOGRAPHY

This list is only a pointer to some books that are essential for anyone interested in ballet. There are many books on individual dancers or important figures in the story of ballet. You will find them in most libraries; ask the librarian if you have any difficulty.

Ambrose, Kay, *Classical Dances and Costumes of India.*
Beaumont, C. W., *The Complete Book of Ballets* (also its sequels, *Supplement to the Complete Book, Ballet Past and Present, etc.*)
––– *The Diaghilev Ballet in London.*
––– *Ballet Design Past and Present.*
Beaumont, C. W., and Idzikowski, Stanislas, *A Manual of Classical Theatrical Dancing.*
Brunelleschi, Elsa, *Antonio.*
Chujoy, Anatole, *The New York City Ballet.*
Clarke Mary, *The Sadler's Wells Ballet.*
––– *Dancers of Mercury.*
Cohen, S. J., and Pischl, A. J., *American Ballet Theatre.*
Dandre, Victor, *Anna Pavlova.*
De Mille, Agnes, *Dance to the Piper.*
––– *To A Young Dancer.*
De Valois, Ninette, *Invitation to the Ballet.*
––– *Come Dance with Me.*
Drew, David, ed., *The Decca Book of Ballet.*
Franks, A. H., *Twentieth Century Ballet.*
Gautier, Théophile, *The Romantic Ballet,* trans. by C. W. Beaumont.

Guest, Ivor, *The Dancer's Heritage* (A Short History of Ballet).
Haskell, Arnold L., *Ballet*.
———*Dancing Round the World*.
Karsavina, Tamara, *Theatre Street*.
——— *Ballet Technique*.
Lawson, Joan, and Revitt, Peter, *Dressing for the Ballet*.
Lloyd, Margaret, *The Borzoi of Modern Dance*.
Markova, Alicia, *Giselle and I*.
Martin, John, *Introduction To The Dance*.
Noverre, Jean Georges, *Letters on Dancing and Ballets,* trans. by
    C. W. Beaumont.
Scott, A. C., *The Classical Theatre of China*.
——— *The Kabuki Theatre of Japan*.
Terry, Walter, *The Dance in America*.

Dictionary of Modern Ballet edited by S. J. Cohen.
Dictionary of Ballet by G. B. L. Wilson.

Index

INDEX

Index